MATTHEW

MATTHEW

The King
and His Kingdom:
God's Rule and Reign
in My Life

David E. Schroeder

Christian Publications
3825 Hartzdale Drive, Camp Hill, PA 17011

Faithful, biblical publishing since 1883

ISBN: 0-87509-605-0
LOC Catalog Card Number: 95-68989
©1995 by Christian Publications, Inc.
All rights reserved
Printed in the United States of America

95 96 97 98 99 5 4 3 2 1

Cover design by Robert Baddorf

For
Lenora, here and now,
and
E.H., then and there

CONTENTS

The *Deeper Life Pulpit Commentary* progresses to two volumes by the publication of *The King and His Kingdom: God's Rule and Reign in My Life*. The first volume in the series was Paul Bubna's work on Second Corinthians, *Ministry: God at Work in Me for the Good of Others*.

Clearly, the preparation and publication of an entire commentary series is a major, long-term undertaking. Moreover, there are already more commentaries of every type and style than anyone can reasonably use. So why another series? Why another commentary on Matthew?

We believe that with succeeding volumes this series will more and more clearly claim an important niche in the ranks of evangelical commentaries. It will justify and distinguish itself by three characteristics:

1. its expository soundness
2. its homiletical framework
3. its emphasis on the deeper life

No other series has this combination of concerns. And the authors chosen are proven ministers of the Word and uniquely qualified to fulfill the promise of the project.

The target audience for this series is the professional or lay student of Scripture who seeks a deeper Christian life. Pastor/teachers may use it to help them frame sermons and presentations that exhort their people to greater maturity. Lay students of Scripture will value it for its engaging style and compelling value, leading them to a greater knowledge of and a deeper walk with the God of the Bible.

Because the authors and the biblical materials vary, the reader may expect to find some diversity of style in the series. Some pithy sections may be handled in a verse-by-verse format; others more thematic may be covered with broader strokes. Future volumes in the series will strive for a gracious balance between standardization and individual style of each author.

Finally, a word about this particular volume. *The Gospel According to Matthew* has been called the *Gospel of the Kingdom*. Teaching about the kingdom of God was the centerpiece of the oral ministry of Jesus. His first message and His last were about the kingdom. His famous parables were about the kingdom. The kingdom is that which we are to "seek first."

Assuming that no author of Scripture spoke or wrote more profoundly than Jesus, we may also assume that His main theme was the closest to the heart of God and that which would draw His hearers deepest into the knowledge of God. Understanding and conforming to the kingdom of God are probably the two most challenging and important tasks of the Christian life. Matthew's Gospel, therefore, must be among the most essential documents any follower of Christ will ever encounter. May the insights and illumination of this volume be used by God to draw you deeper into the kingdom.

The Matthew Mystique

If I asked you what was the first written book of the New Testament, what would you answer? No, it was not Matthew. New Testament scholars generally agree that the first written book of the New Testament was either the book of James or one of Paul's writings, depending on your view of the writing of the epistle to the Galatians. But certainly it was not Matthew.

If I asked you who wrote the first Gospel, what would you answer? Matthew? Perhaps, but not likely. Several schools of thought exist in regard to the order in which the Gospels were written, but the general consensus is that Mark's Gospel was written first.

Now, if I asked you who wrote the Gospel presented first in the New Testament, what would you answer? If you say "Matthew," you would probably be correct. I say "probably" for several reasons. First, although the "Gospel According to Matthew" is the first Gospel presented in the

New Testament, it is in reality an anonymous Gospel. Second, historical testimony attributes this book to the disciple named Matthew. Our main purpose, however, is not to challenge this idea, but to help you become a more keen observer of the text by looking at the internal evidence (that is, what is actually said) in the book. By internal evidence we really do not have a clue as to who its author may have been. Fortunately, the early church fathers, who quoted this Gospel more frequently than any other, unanimously credit Matthew as its author. Later I will present another interesting hypothesis that has some support by an early church father. The main point here is to get you to sharpen your eye as a keen observer of the text.

Eyewitness Reporting

Suppose for a moment that you are a second generation Christian, living in what we now consider to be the second half of the first century A.D. Rather than living in Your Town, USA, you live in Jerusalem. Most of your compatriots are Jewish and believe that the Jesus Movement is a heretical, unorthodox sect. After all, Christians believe in things such as the plurality of gods (the Trinity), God becoming a man, the God-man dying on a cursed tree at the hands of heathens and the remarkable claim that He rose from the dead and ascended to heaven.

As a Christian believer, you firmly hold that Jesus, your Messiah, is the fulfillment of the Old Covenant promises and predictions. But you have neither first-hand evidence nor a written record of the life and teachings of the Messiah, and all of the eyewitnesses are dying off. What would be your most urgent need? No doubt, you would want one of the eyewitnesses to leave behind a written account of his experiences and remembrances of Jesus the Messiah.

Who would be most qualified to meet that need? Surely, those who lived closest to Jesus and observed His life and remembered His teachings. The early church called these men apostles. All four Gospels have apostolic credentials. Matthew himself was an apostle. Mark's Gospel is said to have been influenced greatly by Peter. Luke's Gospel is said to have been influenced greatly by Paul and others. (While Paul was not one of the original Twelve, the early church considered him to be an apostle. The prelude to Luke's Gospel [1:1-4] indicates that he based his material on many eyewitness accounts.) And certainly John was an apostle.

The dating of the four Gospels is generally considered to be between 60 and 85 A.D., 30 to 55 years after Jesus ascended.

Besides wanting to retain a living memory of the events and teachings of Jesus, what are other reasons for having a written account? Seven ideas come to mind:

1. Christianity was advancing into educated, literate cultures throughout the known world. By recording the life and teachings of Jesus in the

Greek language, which was nearly a universal language, many more people would hear the wonderful message.

2. Parents desired to teach their children about Jesus. They could use the oral tradition of their culture, but having written accounts that could be read during church services would be extremely helpful in the work of educating their children in the Christian faith.

3. Many strange and heretical ideas about Jesus were being circulated. A written account would provide an objective standard against heresy.

4. Christians were convinced that Jesus was the fulfillment of the Old Testament promises for a Messiah. A written gospel would provide ample evidence of their claims and be useful for apologetic purposes.

5. During public church services, especially during the sharing of the Lord's Supper, it would be very helpful to have readings about the life and teachings of the Lord.

6. As important as a recounting of the life story of Jesus may have been, the early Christians had a particular reverence for the sayings of Jesus. While long-term memory and oral tradition were useful, the sayings of Jesus were of such importance, being in fact the Word of God that the early

believers wanted the words in writing.

7. Now that the early Christians understood that Jesus Himself was the New Covenant, they realized that an account of His life and death and subsequent writings by the apostles would form a complementary body to the old covenant (Old Testament).

Maybe you can think of other reasons why, as a first-century Christian, you would have desired a written account of the life and teachings of Jesus. Surely, if you could have looked down the corridors of time and seen the great impact the Gospels would make, you would have been even more eager for Matthew and the others to pick up their quills and begin to write.

Structure and Purpose

Have you ever noticed in your reading and study of the Gospels that they record various events in different orders? For example, John tells us that Jesus cleansed the temple in Jerusalem in the early days of His ministry (John 2:13). Matthew, Mark and Luke, however, relate that Jesus cleansed the temple a day or so after His triumphal entry into Jerusalem, shortly before His crucifixion (Matthew 21:12-13; Mark 11:15-17; Luke 19:45-46). Perhaps He cleansed the temple on two separate occasions, or maybe even more than twice. Without objective, internal evidence, however, it is difficult to be dogmatic.

The Gospel writers record many other events in apparently different chronological sequences. The first three Gospels, that is, Matthew, Mark and Luke, are often called the "synoptic Gospels." The word synoptic, which means *able to be seen together*, suggests that these three Gospels take a very similar approach to recording the life and teachings of Jesus. The fact that they share much parallel material supports this.

Yet a closer look at the synoptic Gospels indicates that Mark and Luke seem to agree on the chronology of the events of the life of Jesus, whereas Matthew's sequence is quite different. As a historian, Luke makes a special effort to indicate that he was setting down a chronological account. Luke 1:3 says, "Therefore, since I myself have carefully investigated everything from the beginning, it seemed good also to me to write an orderly account . . ." The words *orderly account* may also be translated *in consecutive order* (NASV).

You might ask, "If Luke and Mark chose to write chronologically, why would Matthew not do the same?" New Testament scholars generally agree that both Matthew and John wrote thematically. While a general historical chronology exists in all four Gospels, the theological and thematic development seen in Matthew and John is quite evident. The structure of Matthew's Gospel resembles that of plywood, in which six layers of narrative alternate with five layers of teaching material. Also, notice that Matthew uses the word "finished" in a formula to conclude each teaching section (see 7:28, 11:1, 13:53, 19:1, and 26:1). The basic formula says, "When Jesus had finished saying these things . . ." (7:28), or "When Jesus had finished these parables . . ." (13:53), or something very similar. In fact, this commentary will follow that same structure (see the table of contents).

What was Matthew's purpose for writing his Gospel, especially if he wasn't primarily concerned about the chronology of the life of Jesus? Three ideas seem to emerge.

First, Matthew was eager to show the continuity between the Old Testament and the mission of Jesus as the Messiah. Over and over again, Matthew demonstrates that certain events in Jesus' life were fulfillments of Old Testament Scriptures, and Matthew even quotes those Old Testament Scriptures.

Second, Matthew wrote his material to serve as a polemic against the critics of Jesus. Matthew wanted to present the case for the messiahship of Jesus and refute false, inaccurate claims regarding who He was and what He said. The strongest critics of Jesus in the first century were fellow Jews who would not accept His messiahship.

Third, Matthew wanted to instruct Christians in the ethical implications of their faith. The moral teachings of Jesus set a new standard for people. No longer was adherence to the law of Moses an adequate standard. The earliest teachings of Jesus recorded by Matthew are called the Sermon on the Mount, and in that sermon Jesus gave a new interpretation to long held maxims from the books of the Law.

Without any doubt, the dominant theme of Matthew's Gospel is the *kingdom of heaven*. For Matthew, this does not refer to heaven itself; in fact, the parallel passages in Mark and Luke use the phrase *kingdom of God*. Being sensitive to his Jewish audience, Matthew substituted the word *heaven* for *God*, since devout Jews avoided even pronouncing the name of God so as to not use it in vain. Although Matthew uses both phrases, he favors the phrase *kingdom of heaven*, which occurs 33 times; *kingdom of God* appears only four times. What did he mean by it? The concept of the kingdom of God does not reduce to one simple statement. Indeed, Jesus spent three years of public ministry defining that concept. He did this both through direct teaching and through examples of life. In fact, most of His parables concern some aspect of the kingdom. Some of the parables suggest that the kingdom of God is present and earthly, here and now. Others suggest that it is remote in time and more heavenly, then and there. So which is it? "Here and now" or "then and there"?

When the Pharisees challenged Jesus about the coming of the kingdom of God, He answered them, "The kingdom of God does not come with your careful observation, nor will people say, 'Here it is,' or 'There it is,' because the kingdom of God is within you" (Luke 17:20-21). Jesus thereby affirmed the present reality of the kingdom. Yet other teachings of Jesus clearly show that in this life we know nothing about other future dimensions of the kingdom.

God's kingdom is His presence, power, and authority. When He chooses to confront a situation, that is the kingdom of God. The kingdom of God was most clearly seen when Jesus used His power to defeat the effects of sin in the lives of people. His authority astonished everyone who witnessed His mighty acts and teachings. Luke 11:20 reports an interesting statement of Jesus about the nature of the kingdom. After He had expelled a demon, the Pharisees challenged Him regarding the source of His authority. They suggested that His strength came from the realm of the demonic. Jesus quickly rebutted that foolish notion and then said, "If I drive out demons by the finger of God, then the kingdom of God has come to you."

Thus, Jesus saw and taught that the kingdom of God is a great interruption to the forces of evil and the damning effects of sin on God's creation. Inaugurated in the ministry of Jesus, God's kingdom will overrule every power that would attempt to undermine and diminish the creative work of God. Jesus insisted that His ministry would continue and even be enhanced by the efforts of His followers. "I tell you the truth, anyone who has faith in me will do what I have been doing. He will do even greater things than these, because I am going to the Father" (John 14:12).

Not many of us would claim that our ministries are greater than or even comparable to the ministry of Jesus, but the corporate church of Jesus

Christ has taken the gospel beyond the borders of Palestine and propagated the witness of the gospel in nearly every culture of today's world. Ultimately, the key to demonstrating God's kingdom is the transforming of self-centered sinners (the way we all start out) into God-centered disciples. That is what Jesus prayed for when He said, "Your kingdom come, your will be done on earth as it is in heaven." God's will is done by kingdom people, His disciples.

Special Features of Matthew's Gospel

The Gospel of Matthew was obviously written by a Jew for Jews. Matthew's account implies a knowledge of the Jewish way of life and refers to practices such as almsgiving and fasting. Matthew was very concerned to show that Christianity is the true consummation of the older covenant set up within Judaism. Thus, to demonstrate that Jesus was the fulfillment of prophecy, Matthew frequently told His audience that a certain event was a direct fulfillment of an Old Testament prophecy. (See, for example, 1:22; 2:15, 17, 23; 4:14; 8:17; 12:17; 13:35; 21:4; 26:56 and 27:9.)

Furthermore, Matthew seems to go out of his way to demonstrate that the sect of the Pharisees gave an interpretation of Judaism that resulted in hypocrisy. Without question, Jesus boldly confronted the Pharisees which, within the sovereign plan of God, led to His crucifixion. Jesus exposed Pharisaism in particular since it was the most highly regarded sect of Judaism. People who joined the strict sect of the Pharisees were devout adherents who truly wanted to please God. Unfortunately, the means by which they attempted to please God guided them into a self-righteous, works-oriented religion.

Another feature of Matthew's Gospel is that Jesus is presented as the great teacher in a systematic way. The five great discourses in the sandwiched structure are all rather lengthy discourses.

Also, Matthew is sometimes considered the ecclesiastical Gospel. One scholar suggests that the book was designed to be used within the church to guide Christian teachers in their work. Following the teachings of Jesus, the Great Teacher, Matthew's Gospel offers instruction on the right way of fasting, almsgiving and prayer; Christian rules for marriage and divorce; conduct toward children and others in the faith; the power of the church to make decisions; encouragement for those in times of persecution; authority for baptism; and the ongoing presence of the Lord for even the smallest group of believers who are worshiping. In fact, Matthew is the only Gospel that uses the word *church*, which appears three times—once in 16:18 and twice in 18:17.

Having looked at these special features of the Gospel, let us come back to the question of the book's composition. Papias, an early church father from near the end of the second century A.D., wrote a very insightful and yet perplexing statement: "Matthew composed the Logia in the Hebrew tongue and everyone interpreted them as he was able." What did Papias mean by this statement? The word *Logia* means the *words*, or *teachings*. Scholars have many ideas about Papias' statement, but at a minimum he meant that the discourse or teaching passages of the Gospel were written down very soon after they were uttered, perhaps even during Jesus' lifetime; and they were written by Matthew in the Hebrew or Aramaic language. Perhaps later, while composing the Gospel, he translated those passages into Greek and inserted these teachings between the sections that we call narrative or events, which he also wrote in Greek. This would be one explanation for the unique structure of Matthew.

Some biblical scholars who enjoy extremely detailed analyses of the Gospels are called form critics. They try to determine the precise literary history and formation of the Gospels. Noting a significant amount of parallel material in the synoptic Gospels and also much parallel material between Matthew and Luke, which is nearly all teaching material, they hypothesize that the Gospel writers composed them through normal editorial methods.

We need to remember that nearly 2,000 years separate us from the writing of the original New Testament books. The Christians nearest to the time of writing believed that God's Spirit inspired the human authors; Christians who followed accorded to these books the special status of being canonical. The word *canon* refers to those books that have measured up to a particular standard and, therefore, have been declared to be the Word of God.

Surely, we cannot ignore the involvement of human authors in the recording of Scripture. Yet orthodox Christians affirm that God the Holy Spirit is the ultimate Author of all 66 books of the Bible, regardless of the various methodologies employed by the human writers that He inspired.

Let us now consider this gospel of the kingdom.

CHAPTER 1

The Kingdom Unveiled

Matthew 1-4

Several years ago an interesting and probably quite healthy craze appeared in America. People eagerly began to trace their roots by studying their family's genealogy. Libraries and courthouses were flooded with people trying to connect with their family's past. I know of one family that even arranged their vacations to study the history of their forbears both in this country and in Europe.

In first-century Judaism, such studies were unnecessary. Genealogies in the days of Jesus were scrupulously kept. Thus, Matthew begins his Gospel with the phrase, "A record of the genealogy of Jesus Christ . . . ."

The Infancy Narrative (Matthew 1-2)

Chapters 1 and 2 of Matthew are called the infancy narrative. You may have noticed in your study of the Gospels that only Matthew and Luke really tell us much about the early days of Jesus on earth. Mark skips over the first 30 years of Jesus' life and introduces Jesus through the ministry of John the Baptist. The Apostle John, in his philosophical and theological way, introduces Jesus as the Word that was with God from the beginning, but just like Mark, John fast-forwards to the ministry of Jesus, skipping altogether the infancy and childhood days of Jesus.

The Pedigree of the Messiah (1:1-17)

Matthew's Jewish orientation is evident in that he begins the lineage of Jesus with Abraham, the father of the Jewish people. Luke's more universal interest takes the lineage of Jesus back to Adam.

As mentioned above, the Jews and particularly the Sanhedrin kept scrupulous records about a person's lineage. In those days it was extremely important to determine whether a person was a purebred Jew. The hostilities between Jews and Samaritans, who were considered half-breed Jews, motivated the Pharisees especially to pursue this purity of their race.

As Matthew shows the lineage, we see an interesting numerical arrangement: 14 names from Abraham to David; another 14 from David to the exile; and then Matthew shows another 14 generations from after the deportation to Babylon until the time of Jesus. We see this summarized in Matthew 1:17.

Many of the names in this lineage are famous.

Quite noteworthy is the mention of a number of women with dubious backgrounds. Verse three mentions Tamar. She was Judah's daughter-in-law who, after her husband died and none of his brothers were fulfilling the law by taking her as a wife, conspired to seduce Judah. Dressing as a harlot, she attracted his attention and became impregnated by him. Months later when her pregnancy was detected, she exonerated herself by showing Judah's ring, cords and staff, which she had stolen for the purpose of demonstrating that the child she was carrying was indeed her father-in-law's. Thus, she was exonerated and considered to be more righteous than Judah who had withheld his youngest son from her.

Rahab, a Canaanite harlot, is mentioned. Of course, she was David's great-grandmother. Another Gentile woman mentioned in the genealogy of Jesus is Ruth, who was the grandmother of David. If you know her story, you remember her as a godly person. Also, you recognize how rich was young David's spiritual heritage.

Finally, we find Bathsheba in the list. Although her name is not actually mentioned, the text does refer to "the wife of Uriah." Why Matthew chose not to list her actual name is an interesting question. Perhaps he was trying to keep the reader's attention on the genealogy and not add distraction by what surely was one of the more startling and controversial aspects of the life of the greatest Jewish king.

Nevertheless, part of Matthew's intention in

listing the genealogy is to show that the Messiah
had come through a lineage that was quite offensive to Jewish scruples. Many of the barriers that
some of the fastidious Jews proudly erected were
already being demolished even in this genealogy
of the Messiah. Matthew is telling us that not just
Jews are acceptable, for Gentiles also play a role in
God's plan. Not just males are acceptable, but fe-
males, too. Not just so-called saints are acceptable,
but sinners, also. Thus, the pedigree of the Messiah includes the very kind of people He came to
seek and to save.

The Birth of the Messiah (1:18-25)

What did Matthew intend in relating the details
of Jesus' birth? For one thing, he certainly wanted
to establish the legitimacy of Christ's birth. The
best way to do this for a Jewish audience was to
show the connection between His birth and the
prophecies of old.

Five times in chapters 1 and 2, Matthew cites
Old Testament prophecies that were being fulfilled in the birth of Jesus. To affirm the virgin
birth of Jesus, Matthew quotes Isaiah 7:14, "The
virgin will be with child and will give birth to a
son, and they will call him Immanuel." Matthew
then affirms that, "All this took place to fulfill
what the Lord had said through the prophet." The
birthplace of Jesus was also a fulfillment of prophecy. Matthew cites Micah 5:2, which predicted the
Messiah would be born in lowly Bethlehem of
Judea, ". . . for this is what the prophet has writ-

ten" (Matthew 2:5). Also, Matthew used Hosea 11:1 to demonstrate that the escape to Egypt was a fulfillment of Old Testament prophecy. He quoted Jeremiah 31:15 to demonstrate that the slaughter of infants in Bethlehem was also the fulfillment of prophecy. And then, even though the Old Testament reference is uncertain, Matthew shows that by living in Nazareth, Jesus "fulfilled what was said through the prophets: 'He will be called a Nazarene' " (Matthew 2:23).

Reading the story of Jesus' birth impresses on us the lowly and humble circumstances into which He was born. One would have expected a Messiah to have been born to royalty; not so with Jesus. In fact, Mary and Joseph are not even middle-class people. They are among the poorest of the poor. We can sense a sympathetic and even pastoral heart in the author of the Gospel as he takes us through the trauma of a young maiden found to be pregnant and her espoused husband, also a virgin, having to grapple with her claim of innocence. Fortunately, God Himself stepped into this tense situation giving an angelic visitation to Joseph. Joseph certainly was a New Testament hero. While undoubtedly few young maidens would have had the nobility of character to have been chosen by God to be the mother of the Messiah, so it must be true that few young men would have had that same spirit to have been chosen to give parental guidance to a child considered to be of questionable conception. We can only wonder how much faith was inspired in Joseph when he heard the angel announce that the name of the child should be Jesus, "because he will save his people from their sins" (Matthew 1:21).

The theological significance of this birth is impossible to overestimate. Two great doctrines have their roots in this narrative. First, the great concept of the incarnation, God taking on human flesh through the life of a naturally born baby, was certainly a preposterous notion. It still is. First century Jews were not the only ones to stumble on this truth claim. The idea seems absurd from two standpoints. The thought that God Almighty, the Creator and Ruler of the universe, would reduce Himself to human frailty seems preposterous. C.S. Lewis suggests that if we want to try to identify with this great condescension, we ought to imagine what it might be like for us suddenly to be changed into a slug or an earthworm. Even that condescension does not adequately describe the great humbling of the Son of God to become a human being.

Another stumbling block in the incarnation for many people is that the child was born in the same manner as any other child. This was no "special delivery." The embryo grew in Mary's womb. The birth came through her canal just as any other human birth. No doubt, Jesus was spanked on the bottom and began to cry to take His first breath. And certainly, before too many hours, Mary and Joseph found themselves dealing with all of the mundane chores that all new parents experience, from regular feedings to changing diapers. The offense of God taking on Himself the animal part of our being seems preposterous. The word incarnation comes from the Latin word *carne*, the word for *meat* or *flesh*. God has taken on our flesh.

The second great theological truth that Matthew affirms here is that Jesus was born of a virgin. Unfortunately, confidence in this doctrine seems to be eroding even among so-called evangelicals. Is the virgin birth one of the cardinal, or essential, fundamentals of the faith? Some may rightly argue that the writers of the epistles do not greatly emphasize the virgin birth of Jesus. Is that because they did not believe it or because the fact was so widely known and assumed among the Christian community that the point did not need to be belabored? Surely the latter is the case. To suggest to a first-century disciple that Joseph was the biological father of Jesus would have produced scorn.

Yes, the virgin birth of Jesus is a fundamental part of orthodox faith. As the second Adam, His innocence was every bit as pure as the first Adam's prior to the fall. Matthew's genealogy ends by saying, "[to] Joseph, the husband of Mary, of whom was born Jesus, who is called Christ" (Matthew 1:16). Thus, Matthew's purpose is to demonstrate the messiahship of Jesus, the word Christ being the same word as Messiah. Luke, however, not so interested in the Jewish genealogy, mentions that Jesus "was the son, so it was thought, of Joseph" (Luke 3:23), and then traces the fathers all the way back to Adam, who is called the "son of God." The prior verse in Luke shows Jesus being baptized and a voice from heaven saying, "You are my Son, whom I love; with you I am well pleased" (Luke 3:22).

The point about the virgin birth is that the genealogy of Jesus goes back to God Himself, who sired His Son, Jesus the Messiah. The theological significance of this is that while being fully human because of his birth from a woman, Jesus also was a fully divine being conceived by God Himself. Thus, because of His supernatural conception, Jesus remained different from the human family in one essential way, namely, He did not have our original sin. Had Jesus been conceived by Joseph or any other man, He would not have been a fully innocent, spotless or perfect substitutionary sacrifice. The doctrine of the atonement is absolutely dependent upon the doctrine of the virgin birth. When evangelicals and others begin to doubt the importance of the doctrine of the virgin birth, they are tampering with the most essential aspect of their faith, namely, the validity of the atonement of Jesus Christ.

By tainting the doctrine of the atonement we, in turn, undermine the doctrine of justification. Without a perfect sacrifice for our sins, God would have had no basis for acquitting our guilt; therefore, our justification would be in question.

While the falling domino kind of mentality does not appeal to me, logically and theologically we must admit that the domino effect does pertain here. By knocking over the doctrine of the virgin birth, we begin to push over the doctrine of the atonement and then the doctrine of justification. Once justification has fallen, what is left of Christian truth and faith that is of any value?

The Visit of the Magi (2:1-12)

Matthew is the only Gospel writer to report the visit of the magi to worship the newborn Christ child. We know that the magi were probably astrologers from the East who had determined through various calculations that an outstanding event was about to occur in Judea. From quotes by the Roman historians Suetonius and Tacitus, William Barclay shows the air was filled with anticipation just about the time when Jesus was born. Many expected a world ruler to come on the scene, and they particularly expected him to come out of Judea. Even the Jewish historian Josephus mentions that his people believed that one was coming who would soon be governor over all of the habitable earth.

These astrologers, who perhaps were Midian priests, ran into the paranoid personality of Herod who was almost insanely suspicious. Having murdered his wife, his mother-in-law, his eldest son and two other sons, Herod certainly was not about to tolerate any rival king. Thus, he was eager to be alerted to the findings of the astrologers. God actively intervened in the situation and warned the magi in a dream not to return to Herod.

Likewise, God warned Joseph through an angel in a dream to take his young family and flee to the land of Egypt. As in every other instance, Joseph obeyed the message he received from the Lord. Unfortunately, not all the other young parents in Bethlehem were privy to such a warning. In his rage, Herod slaughtered all the young males of Bethlehem who were two years and younger. Historians suggest that Herod's henchmen killed perhaps 30 to 40 babies. It is amazing to what extent people will go to be free from Christ or any other rival claim to their personal sovereignty.

One of the most wonderful experiences for a pastor is dedicating babies. Often when counseling young parents, I have helped them understand that the dedication of the baby is less meaningful apart from the dedication of the parents to God's sovereign work in the life of their child. Certainly, the young parents in Bethlehem who lost their young sons paid an awfully great price without ever understanding why. Those who faithfully submitted to the sovereignty of God, like many other bereaved parents throughout history, were able to overcome the pain and grief suffered by the loss. Unfortunately, those parents who became bitter toward God, foolishly joined the ranks of Herod by rebelling against God's sovereign purposes.

From Egypt to Nazareth (2:13-23)

Having lived in Egypt for some time, Joseph moved his young family back to the land of his people and was warned by God to settle in the northern country of Galilee. Thus, Jesus grew up in the town of Nazareth. Never again do we hear about Joseph. He probably died sometime during Jesus' childhood, requiring Jesus as the oldest son to support his family.

Preparation for Ministry (Matthew 3-4)

The only information we have about Jesus between His days of infancy and the beginning of His ministry is given by Luke, who offers a very brief sketch of an incident when 12-year-old Jesus and His family were visiting Jerusalem. The story ends with an insightful statement about Jesus' development: "And Jesus grew in wisdom and stature, and in favor with God and men" (Luke 2:52). While we may wish to know more about the childhood and adolescence of Jesus, it is apparently not essential for us to know.

The Ministry of John the Baptist (3:1-12)

Two episodes in John's preparation for ministry give us very important insights into the spirit and character of Jesus. Chapter 3 begins by introducing John the Baptist who we know from other accounts was a cousin of Jesus. Whether the two knew each other prior to this event in the wilderness of Judea, we cannot say for certain. Some scholars have speculated that John lived his childhood in the Essene community and may well have been separate from the community in which Jesus was raised.

Certainly John knew his own identity and mission. He came first as a preacher calling on the Jews to repent and preaching the nearness of the kingdom of heaven. Surely this was a radical thought for Jewish people. Some of the more humble ones might have accepted the need for repentance, but to affirm that the kingdom of heaven was at hand was quite another thing. Jewish eschatology called for a sudden, decisive and climactic "day of the Lord," when God would suddenly appear to destroy the enemies of Israel and set up the throne of David with a conquering Messiah to rule over Israel. The presence of a kingdom certainly was not recognized within Israel.

Even more radical was John's insistence that the repentant Jews needed to be baptized. Baptism was fine for Gentile proselytes who wanted to accept the Jewish way of life, but the sign of being part of the faithful was circumcision, not baptism. Matthew 3:6 indicates, however, that many were baptized by John in the Jordan River as they confessed their sins. Some of them were Pharisees and Sadducees. John was a bit harsh on them calling them a "brood of vipers" (3:7) and insisting that baptism by itself was not enough. He required them to produce fruit in their lives, which would come out of the humility of repentance. More specifically, he took away from them one of the pinnacles of their pride. He told them in 3:9 that there were no grandchildren in the kingdom of heaven. Claiming Abraham as their father would gain them no merit with God. The only evidence of a right standing with God was the fruit produced in one's life. In fact, verse 10 indicates that a judgment was already going on in which an ax was being wielded in the garden grove, and only those trees that were producing good fruit were spared.

As impressive as John was, he always insisted that One far greater than he was about to appear. John affirmed that he was not even worthy to carry the sandals of this One who would come. Although water baptism for repentance was important, the One who was coming would baptize people with the Holy Spirit and fire. But the Coming One would also bring judgment. John changes part of the imagery by saying that the Coming One would fan the threshing floor, separating the wheat from the chaff. The consistent element in the images in verses 10-12 is fire. The unfruitful trees would be thrown into the fire, the Coming One would baptize people with fire, and He would also "burn up the chaff" with unquenchable fire." (3:12). How are we to understand this image? The focus here seems to be not so much on punishment as on purity. Verse 11 surely is not about punishment because fire is used there in a positive sense. John's sermon indicates that Israel needed to be purified and the Coming One was prepared to do that.

Identifying with the Jewish Renewal Movement (3:13-17)

Then the Coming One appeared. Matthew simply tells us that Jesus came from Galilee to the Jordan to be baptized by John. Recognizing him, John was reluctant to baptize Jesus. However, Jesus insisted on being baptized by John, saying that "It is proper for us to do this to fulfill all righteousness" (Matthew 3:15).

The baptism of Jesus confounds many theologians. If John's baptism was, as he said, a baptism for the repentance and remission of sin, why would Jesus who was sinless receive such baptism? Would it not be viewed by onlookers that Jesus Himself sensed the need for cleansing? Why would He join the ranks of other sinners and submit to this somewhat unorthodox ritual? The following two ideas may help us understand.

First, observe that immediately after Jesus was baptized, heaven was opened and the Spirit of God descended on Jesus like a dove and an audible voice from heaven said, "This is my Son, whom I love; with him I am well pleased." We assume that this heavenly message was for the listening crowd. Could it be, however, that the message was also for Jesus?

Might it be that in reality this occasion was really the first temptation of Jesus? Would He be humble enough to identify with sinners going into the waters of baptism? Perhaps that is what Jesus meant when He said, "It is proper for us to do this to fulfill all righteousness." Having thus humbled Himself, Jesus demonstrated the route He would choose in His ministry—namely, identifying with sinners—and thus the Father exonerated him and reaffirmed that relationship, commending Jesus with the words, "This is my Son, whom I love; with him I am well pleased."

Second, let us remember that John represented something quite new in Judaism. We are not stretching the point to say that he initiated a renewal movement within Jewish religion. His ministry would cause the separation between sober, proud Jews, who saw no need to repent, and those who recognized that their family lineage and nationality were not sufficient to give them an authentic relationship with God.

In reality, John brought about a first-century reformation. Whereas the traditional religious faith seemed to depend on external conditions—Jewishness, circumcision and adherence to the law—John came preaching a message of inner transformation that began with repentance.

As we see later in his ministry, Jesus used John as a decisive dividing line within Judaism. Being insidiously tested by enemies who wanted to trap Jesus into heresy, in Mark 11:30 Jesus asked, "John's baptism—was it from heaven, or from men? Tell me!" Jesus insisted that they take a stand on this critical issue. In so doing, He forced on them the following dilemma: (1) speak out against John, which would not have been popular to do; or (2) identify personally with John's movement, which they also did not want to do.

We suggest here that another reason Jesus

submitted to the baptism of John was to declare to the Jewish nation that He readily identified with the Jewish renewal movement which was occurring. He affirmed John's message of the need to repent and humbly submit to baptism, and by example he led the way into those waters for millions of Christians who subsequently would repent and humbly be buried with Jesus in the waters of baptism.

Resisting Temptation (4:1-11)

Matthew then moves to an even more dramatic moment in the life of Jesus. As humans we are greatly intrigued by stories that pit absolute evil against absolute good. No episode was ever more dramatic in that regard than the temptation of Jesus in the desert. Seizing upon the moment of vulnerability after Jesus had fasted 40 days and nights, Satan first tempted Jesus about His physical hunger. Challenging Jesus to prove He was the Son of God, Satan assured Jesus that He would be doing a good thing by turning stones into bread. Can we doubt at all that this is the same voice that spoke to Eve in the Garden of Eden, offering not bread but fruit?

Passing that part of the test, Jesus was then tempted to demonstrate that He truly was the Son of God by throwing Himself down from the pinnacle of the temple. Using Scripture, and a messianic Psalm at that, Satan assured Jesus that He would be rescued by angels. Again, Jesus responded using Scripture telling Satan not to put "the Lord your God to the test." Isn't it interesting that Satan did not try to argue with Jesus about whether He was "the Lord your God"?

We might wonder what was at stake in this for Satan. What difference would it have made to him if Jesus had turned stones into bread or jumped from the pinnacle of the temple? In the third temptation we see very clearly the motive of Satan. Taking Jesus to a high mountain, he showed Him all the kingdoms of the world and their splendor and then said that he would give these kingdoms to Jesus if He would bow down and worship him. Isn't it interesting that Satan claimed ownership of all the kingdoms of the world? More fascinating is the fact that Jesus did not challenge him about this. In a very real sense, because the kingdoms of the world are held in the grip of sin, Satan does exercise a partial reign over the kingdoms.

It is also noteworthy that Satan was willing to sacrifice all the kingdoms of the world if Jesus would bow down and worship him. We can almost hear him singing, "Take the world but give me Jesus." Satan had enough sense to value Jesus more than he valued the world. Would that more Christians had that same sense.

At this point, using a Scripture from Deuteronomy for the third time, Jesus merely banished Satan. Surely, the use of Scripture in times of temptation is one of the great lessons from the temptation episode.

Another way of understanding the temptations is through the phrases used by the Apostle John in First John 2:16. After telling us not to love the world or the things in the world, John wrote that all that is in the world, "the lust of the flesh and the lust of the eyes and the boastful pride of life" (NASV), is not from the Father but is from the world. These are the three areas in which Satan attempted to seduce Jesus—an appeal to His flesh, His eyes and His pride.

Because we are all prone to succumbing to temptation, it might be helpful to see the enemy's tactic here. Were these temptations so different from the kinds that we suffer? Looking more closely, we see that Satan appealed to pleasure, pride and power—three areas where we are extremely vulnerable. He appealed to the body by offering bread, to the soul by offering popularity and to the spirit by offering glory. In various times in our lives we are apt to succumb to temptations in any of these three areas.

What was really at stake here? Were these real temptations or not? Would it have been possible for Jesus to have sinned? These questions have perplexed many theologians. Fortunately, they are theoretical and moot. At stake, however, was the issue about how Jesus would use His power. Would He use His supernatural abilities for self-centered purposes? How would Jesus achieve notoriety? He knew that part of His mission demanded that He would be a public figure. How would He achieve that fame? Surely, jumping off the pinnacle of the temple only to be caught by angels would be a shortcut to that goal. Also, how much value did Jesus place on winning the world? Would that be more important than being in right relation to the Father? Presumably, Jesus had the freedom to abuse His power. It seems that we are always tempted most strongly through our gifts, and so it was with Jesus.

Pastoring the Kingdom Flock (4:12-25)

By resisting Satan's appeals, Jesus made a statement regarding His ministry style. In fact, Matthew demonstrates that style in 4:12-25. We see Jesus preaching the kingdom of God, calling disciples to follow Him, and healing individuals who were suffering from various diseases. In other words, Jesus began to minister as a humble pastor. He preached the gospel of the kingdom, He called others to follow Him, He assured them that He would make them fishers of men, and He touched people with healing. In all instances, He rendered selfless ministry.

Surely, Jesus unveiled the kingdom, first as an infant with magi adoring Him, then as a candidate for baptism with people sensing His humility, then as a spiritual warrior being tempted by His greatest enemy and then as a pastor ministering to His people. In each instance, the coming of Jesus brought great blessing to this earth. Surely this kingdom would be the culmination of God's great eternal plan.

CHAPTER 2

Principles of the Kingdom

Matthew 5-7

One of the most famous sections of Scripture is the great Sermon on the Mount recorded in Matthew chapters 5 through 7. While these chapters represent a fairly lengthy discourse, the sermon may be read in about 12 minutes. Therefore, it certainly was a short, but powerful sermon. Many of the verses in these three chapters have parallels scattered throughout the Gospel of Luke, especially Luke 6.

For whom was this great sermon intended? Some scholars have suggested that it was addressed primarily to pre-Christian Judaism and that its teachings are irrelevant to those in the age of the church. Known as dispensationalism, this conception of history and theology divides history into different eras or "dispensations" and maintains that God worked out His plan of redemption in different ways in each dispensation. Partitioning Scripture so rigidly and distinguishing which passages are or are not relevant to the people of God, however, is an unwarranted imposition on the biblical text. Dispensational thought makes somewhat arbitrary decisions about the intended audience of various sections of Scripture. Surely, the "all Scripture" of Second Timothy 3:16 becomes a problem for dispensationalism.

Similarly, other scholars believe that the original recipients of the teaching were the pre-Christian followers of Jesus. Obviously, the early disciples were pre-Christian in the sense that the full Christian experience was not yet available prior to the death and resurrection of Jesus. But to assert that the teachings were given for only a pre-Christian audience, and, therefore, should not apply to Christian believers is another unwarranted assumption.

A third possibility is that the sermon was given to millennial people, that is, the teachings are idealistic and refer to the kingdom of God that will be fully realized during the millennium. Understanding the current age to be merely a prelude to the great era yet to come, adherents to this approach assume that these teachings are beyond Christian possibility.

A fourth, and we believe correct, understanding of the original audience is evident in Matthew's own introduction: "Now when he saw the crowds, he went up on a mountainside and sat down. His disciples came to him, and he began to teach them . . ." (Matthew 5:1-2). Clearly, the audience consisted not only of Jesus' disciples, but also of crowds who were sitting on the fringes of the congregation, perhaps eavesdropping. The disciples at this time were Jewish, pre-Christian, but they were also people committed to Jesus and eager to hear His teaching. They had already gained the sense that He spoke with new authority. Others listening to the same sermon would also gain that new sense. Summarizing the sermon, Matthew says, "When Jesus had finished saying these things, the crowds were amazed at his teaching, because he taught as one who had authority, and not as their teachers of the law" (7:28-29).

Qualities for Disciples (Matthew 5:1-12)

Perhaps no part of Scripture has received more written commentary than this great sermon. Our purpose here is not to give a verse-by-verse exposition, but to provide an understanding of the basic principles Jesus taught. The structure of the sermon seems to be threefold: (1) the Beatitudes and subsequent verses (5:1-16) focus on qualities for disciples; (2) the rest of chapter 5 shows Jesus giving a spiritually focused understanding of the Mosaic law; (3) chapters 6 and 7 expose six elements of false religion.

As we approach the introduction to this great sermon, we come to a familiar passage known as the Beatitudes. If the Sermon on the Mount may be considered to be the "constitution of the kingdom," the Beatitudes might be considered the preamble to that constitution. Each of the eight Beatitudes begins with the same word, which is usually translated *blessed*, or *how happy*, or *how fortunate*. Was Jesus here outlining a way for His followers to achieve the good life? Surely, the point here is not about external happiness. The last of the Beatitudes would surely belie that possibility. Being a blessed person in the Judaic sense was living under a divine benediction or experiencing a spiritually satisfying fortune. Conventional wisdom in those days said that the "blessed ones" were those who were rich, of high social standing in the community, and physically well. On a number of occasions, Jesus denounced that point of view (see, for example, Luke 13:1-5 and the parable of the rich man and Lazarus in Luke 16:19-31).

In the Beatitudes Jesus assured His followers that the blessing of God is evidenced by those who are poor in spirit, who mourn, who are meek, merciful, who hunger and thirst for righteousness, are pure in heart, peacemakers and persecuted because of righteousness. Each of these qualities or positions has an attendant blessing. All of the eight blessings are spiritual in nature; thus, Jesus clearly stated to His followers that both the blessings and the qualities that bring about blessing are not related to the world's value system.

To be poor in spirit is to have certain attitudes toward life that usually describe the economically depressed, namely, dependence rather than self-sufficiency; social humility rather than elitism and snobbery; frugality rather than indulgence and luxury; and transparent character rather than pseudosophistication.[1]

To mourn is to be grieved about a sorrowful condition or the sorry state of the world in general. For the follower of Jesus, mourning begins as the sorrow of repentance over the loss of one's innocence, righteousness and self-respect. But mourning is also the Christlike response to all arenas of life where sin holds power and results in judgment and death.[2]

To be meek is to be gentle, mild, patient and tenderhearted. The word means domesticated, as of a wild animal being tamed for useful purposes. It involves a quiet, willing, cheerful obedience and submission to God that stands in direct contrast to the stubborn, willful rebellion and self-assertiveness of the natural man. It connotes not passiveness but active compliance.[3]

To hunger and thirst for righteousness may be interpreted as having powerful cravings that are theological (as in justification), moral (as in personal behavior) and social (as in civil justice). In the Beatitudes social justice seems to be Jesus' primary concern. His people are those who seek humanity's liberation from sin's oppression; who promote civil rights; and who work for justice in the law courts, integrity in business dealings and honor in home and family affairs.[4]

To be merciful is not only to feel others' pains and problems but also to extend relief. The follower of Jesus is quick to see pain, misery and distress and looks for ways to bring healing, comfort and help. To be merciful is to have compassion for others even when it is inconvenient to do so.[5]

To be pure in heart is to desire one thing. To be pure in heart is to have a simple, sincerely motivated will—no deviousness, no ulterior motives and no baseness. The whole life of the pure in heart, both public and private, is transparent before God and man. Hypocrisy and deceit are abhorrent. The pure in heart are without guile.[6]

To be a peacemaker is to put one's own well-being, reputation and life on the line to be a reconciler. The peacemaker is far more concerned about whole relationships than with the petty issues that divide brothers. Rivalry, competitiveness, social distinctions and self-advancement are abhorrent to the peacemaker who views God's family holistically.[7]

To be persecuted for the sake of righteousness is to suffer personal indignity, ostracism and physical pain at the hands of those who cannot tolerate your example and reminders of righteous conduct. The blessedness of this rejection comes by knowing you are on the side of truth, and that you have borne a faithful witness.[8]

Salt and Light (Matthew 5:13-16)

Following this description of the blessed life, Jesus directly addressed His disciples by describing them as the salt of the earth and the light of the world. Salt was highly valued in the first century because of its ability to penetrate and to preserve, but when its saline quality was weakened, it became worthless. Perhaps Jesus was suggesting to the disciples that they will be effective as salt in the world only as they maintain the purity of the qualities He had just described.

The same emphasis seems to be true with the image of light. The whole purpose of light is to give sight in dark conditions. Like salt, light also penetrates. It illuminates and guides. When that light is obstructed by being put under a bowl, for example, it is of no value. Therefore, Jesus instructed the disciples to make sure that they allowed their light to shine before men. The final result of the disciples functioning as salt and light in the world would be their influence in fighting the decay and darkness that surrounded them. The kingdom of God, based on the qualities called Beatitudes, would be seen as a counterculture[9] in which true disciples do not waver between the ways of the world and the kingdom of God, but clearly maintain their vigor and purity in representing the kingdom.

Disciples and the Law (Matthew 5:17-20)

Whenever a new teacher came on the scene in Judaism, people would immediately want to know his thoughts about the law. Within Judaism there were various schools of thought about the prophets of old and the role of law in the community. In fact, the word law may have meant either the Ten Commandments, the five books of Moses known as the Pentateuch, the Law and the Prophets (which we call the Old Testament) or the oral and scribal law. Clearly at issue in the Sermon on the

Mount is the definition of law. For most Jews of
the day, scribal law was considered to be binding.
Jesus was calling the community back to the great
principles of the law which were found in the five
books of Moses. In fact, throughout the Gospels
we find Jesus clashing on a number of occasions
with scribal law.

William Barclay, in his commentary on the
Gospel of Matthew, demonstrates how the scribes
were able to take a simple principle of life, like
keeping the Sabbath day holy, and amplify it to a
complicated web of petty and burdensome rules.
For example, carrying a burden on the Sabbath
day was forbidden because that would be working. However, a burden needed definition, so the
scribal law clarified it as:

> food equal in weight to a dried fig, enough
> wine for mixing in a goblet, milk enough for
> one swallow, honey enough to put upon a
> wound, oil enough to anoint a small mem-
> ber, water enough to moisten an eye salve,
> paper enough to write a customs house no-
> tice upon, ink enough to write two letters of
> the alphabet, reed enough to make a pen.[10]

Writing was also considered to be work, but the
scribes also defined it as follows:

> He who writes two letters of the alphabet
> with his right or with his left hand, whether
> of one kind or of two kinds, if they are writ-

ten with different inks or in different lan-
guages, is guilty. Even if he should write
two letters from forgetfulness, he is guilty,
whether he has written them with ink or
with paint, red chalk, vitriol, or anything
which makes a permanent mark. Also he
that writes on two walls that form an angle,
or on two tablets of his account book so that
they can be read together is guilty. . . . But if
anyone writes with dark fluid, with fruit
juice, or in the dust of the road, or in sand,
or in anything which does not make a permanent mark, he is not guilty . . . .[11]

This kind of casuistry was regarded by the orthodox Jew to be the essence of true religion and
obedience to God.

Most ardent in following this legalistic system
were the Pharisees, whose name means *the separated ones*. This type of legal, performance-based
religion, resulting in either self-righteousness or
an intolerable sense of guilt, was condemned by
Jesus. When He said in verse 17 that He did not
come to abolish the Law or the Prophets but to
fulfill them, Jesus was not referring to the scribal
law that He continually violated, but the Mosaic
law. Verses 18 and 19 could not be stronger statements of the importance Jesus placed on the Old
Testament Scripture. He affirmed both its prophetic trustworthiness and its binding importance
for demonstrating the kingdom of heaven.

He did not, however, affirm the Pharisees and

teachers of the law; rather, He told the disciples that unless their righteousness would surpass that of the Pharisees and teachers of the law, they would not enter the kingdom of heaven. The obvious implication is that pharisaic, legal righteousness was inadequate. Jesus was not looking for greater conformity to the law—that would be nearly impossible—but rather for an entirely different kind of righteousness. Surely, this should be viewed as an early hint of a distinction between righteousness by works and justification by grace.

Nevertheless, it is impossible to escape the sense that Jesus deliberately set out to redefine the scope of the law. We might ask by what authority He could undertake this seemingly blasphemous task. The reverence that Jews had for the law was such that without proper scribal or rabbinical authority, one risked great censuring for such tampering.

Three ideas may help us understand what Jesus was doing. First, these laws, where they are valid restatements of Old Testament laws, were given for judicial purposes, not for personal morality. For example, the Old Testament law of "an eye for an eye and a tooth for a tooth" was never meant to promote personal revenge. Rather, the injunction was given for judges to execute justice.

Second, the understanding that Jesus brought to the concept of "fulfill" the law is very important. A paraphrase of the verse is that Jesus came to "fill the law full with meaning." Jesus intended for the Jewish community to understand the heart of God who gave the laws in the first place. For example, the law about divorce was intended to demonstrate that God places high value on lifelong marriages.

Third, by using the phrase "But I say unto you" repetitively, Jesus was affirming to the people that His authority was indeed greater than the authority of the writer of the law. On a number of occasions in Scripture the superiority of Jesus over Moses is clearly set forth. This authority certainly convinced the listening audience, "because he taught as one who had authority, and not as their teachers of the law" (Matthew 7:29).

Five False Applications of the Law (Matthew 5:21-48)

Now let us look more closely at the five sections in which Jesus gave a more God-focused understanding of the law. First, Jesus demonstrated that not just the act of murder, but murderous intent violates the spirit of the law. Anger and contempt, being the fruit of the sinful nature, hold one subject to the danger of the fire of hell. God's primary concern is to overcome anger with reconciliation. Therefore, even the act of offering a sacrifice at an altar must be suspended until relationships have been restored. Here as well as many other places in Scripture, God's Word affirms that the relationship between brothers is far more important than the issues that separate them. Kingdom morality was not being observed merely by refraining from

murder. Rather, kingdom morality would be fulfilled when a disciple renounced his anger and
contempt for his brother and sought reconciliation. The law clearly forbade adultery, but
kingdom morality would not be expressed
merely by refraining from the physical act. Jesus
insisted that the lustful intent of committing
adultery was equally as wrong as the fulfillment
of the act itself. The seriousness of the sin of lust
is evidenced by the hyperbolic prescription
given by Jesus—gouging out one of your eyes to
avoid the offense. Clearly, this must be interpreted as hyperbole because it is just as possible
to lust with one eye as it is with two. Jesus'
point is that disciples ought not to take a sin
lightly merely because it is not evident to someone else. If gouging out an eye or dismembering
one's body would enable him to refrain from
further sin, surely, that would be worthwhile in
the spiritual economy of Jesus. Continuing to
lust or sin in some other way makes one a candidate for gehenna or hell fire.

Next comes the issue of divorce. This was a
hot topic in Judaism, and the rabbinical schools
of Hillel and Shammai differed greatly on it.
The former school adopted a liberal, broad-
minded perspective that said if a husband found
anything unfavorable in his wife, he could put
her away by divorce. This could include going
out into public with her head uncovered, or
speaking with another man in the street, or even
ruining a meal. Essentially, if anything dissatis-

fied him with her, he could divorce her. The school of Shammai, however, took a conservative position, insisting that the only legitimate cause for divorce was sexual unfaithfulness. Clearly, Jesus sided with the school of Shammai. More will be said about this subject when we consider Matthew 19:3-9.

Next, Jesus tackled the issue of honesty. The law maintained that a person should not break an oath. If he swore to do something or swore that something was true, then he should back that vow or oath with action. Unfortunately, through tricky manipulation of words, people found ways to get around their vows. For example, rather than swearing by God, a person might swear by invoking the throne of heaven. While this concept may embody the idea of God, the absence of His name would supposedly exempt them from fulfilling their vow. The practice of evading the consequences of a vow reached an art form. The most clever of men could convince someone of his total sincerity and integrity while at the same time leaving himself an out through verbal trickery. Jesus insisted that the heart of the matter was that a person should not have to invoke a vow or an oath since one's word of "Yes" or "No" should be able to be taken with total sincerity and without fear of duplicity.

Next, the law from antiquity suggested that it was legitimate to seek revenge for wrongdoing. While in a fight, if person A caused person B to lose an eye, person B seemingly had the right to retaliate and take an eye from person A. This mentality appealed to people who wanted to take the law into their own hands. For personal ethics, Jesus insisted that far from seeking revenge, a person who has suffered an indignity should overwhelm his opponent with love. The point here, as we will see later in this sermon, is to demonstrate a value system that affirms the other person— even an enemy—as more important than any abuse a disciple might suffer. The value system of the kingdom of God contradicts natural human instincts and calls upon disciples to view other people as God does. Rather than seeing them as enemies or persecutors, disciples must see them as people in great need whom the Father in heaven loves. If God causes the sun to rise on the evil and the good and sends rain upon the righteous and the unrighteous equally, surely it is improper for His children to respond less generously.

What Jesus was calling for here is summed up in the word "perfect" or "mature." The complete person, the mature person, is the one who behaves like the heavenly Father, who Himself is perfectly mature.

In all of these descriptions where Jesus employed the formula "you have heard that it was said . . . but I say unto you," He was teaching kingdom principles of love, honor and integrity. The letter of the law said, "No murder;" the spirit of the law says, "No rage." The letter of the law said, "No adultery;" the spirit of the law says, "No lust." The letter of the law said, "Divorce is permissible;" the spirit of the law says, "Lasting marriages." The letter of the law said, "Fulfill vows;" the spirit of the law says, "Do not make vows." The letter of the law said, "Seek revenge;" the spirit of the law says, "Seek reconciliation."

Clearly, this kingdom calls for a different kind of citizen who lives from the inside out with a divine perspective on virtues and values.

False Religion (Matthew 6:1-18)

Many of Jesus' Jewish peers were living not only according to a false interpretation of the law, but also with false religious practices. In Matthew 6 and 7 Jesus highlighted six areas in which wrong motives and distorted ideals tainted religious life. Specifically, Jesus put his finger on false giving, false praying, false fasting, false security, false counseling and false prophets. In each instance, we will see that the lack of the divine perspective contributed to an inadequate understanding of the role of religion.

Giving alms to the needy appears to be such a charitable and selfless act that one would think it unassailable. Not so. Looking into the hearts of some of His benevolent contemporaries, Jesus saw an unrighteous motive. In fact, Jesus called these philanthropists hypocrites because their primary concern was not the well-being of the poor, but gaining acclaim from others. Both in the synagogues and the streets, these hypocrites sought recognition for their generosity. Jesus affirmed that they would receive a reward, despite their wrong motives. Indeed, other people would pay them high regard. Yet that ought not be the primary consideration for serving God or humanity. If a person's focus is God-ward, he will do all that he can to see that all glory for any good deed goes to the Father. Jesus said that the Father who sees in secret will, in His own time and way, reward the almsgiver.

Likewise, we would think that a virtuous act such as praying could not possibly be distorted. However, Jesus stripped the veneer off this religious exercise and got to the heart of hypocrisy. Some of the more devout Jews distorted this practice in two ways.

First, they would demonstrate their piety by praying aloud in public places in order to be seen by others. Jesus said that they have received their reward in full. We can sense a bit of sarcasm in the comment here because implied in that statement is the fact that their prayers would not be answered. They were rewarded with exactly what they were seeking, namely, to be noticed by others. The prescription Jesus gave is to pray in private, so that the Father can give His special reward to the person who prays in sincerity.

Second, some Jews distorted praying through the vain repetition of words. Perhaps Jesus was attacking the tendency to wax eloquently, piling up silvery language on top of itself so that others would be impressed by the command of thought and word. Perhaps He was also referring to an exaggerated, melodramatic style of praying, in which one's emotions run far ahead of real heart concerns.

By giving what we call the Lord's Prayer, Jesus demonstrated a pattern whose most immediate attribute is simplicity. The phrases are short, the issues are deep, the attitude is one of humility and dependency. The elements of worship, petition and confession dominate the prayer. The priority of God's kingdom is evident, as is the threat of the evil one who would tempt believers away from the priorities of the kingdom. Not often seen in this prayer is a strong statement of social obligation. The request for the forgiveness of debts is followed by the assertion that the one who has prayed has forgiven his debtors. At the conclusion of the prayer, Jesus continued this idea by teaching that prayer for forgiveness can be short-circuited if one is not willing to forgive the sins of others. This idea is not adequately emphasized in our day. Social and theological concerns intersect at this point. Jesus was saying that our relationship to God is affected by our relationships with other humans. In fact, the way He relates to us greatly depends on the way we relate to His other children. Perhaps millions of Christians assume they have been forgiven by God, when in reality they still harbor anger, resentment, bitterness and an unforgiving spirit toward others and thereby never achieve a clean slate with God.

Fasting was a third common religious practice that the hypocrites unfortunately distorted. Wanting to gain recognition for this ascetic practice,

people would at times appear in public quite un-
kempt, showing to others that they were observing a fast. Barclay called this public display "an
ostentatious parade of piety."[12] Like almsgiving
and praying, however, fasting has its proper role
in the spiritual life. For the truly devout person,
the value of fasting is not in the public acclaim
that it gains, but the reward received from the Father, who should be the only audience of fasting.

In each of the three cases we have seen thus far,
Jesus repeated the phrase, "your Father, who sees
what is done in secret, will reward you" (6:4, 6,
18).

Three Warnings (Matthew 6:19-7:23)

Moving away from ascetic religious practices,
Jesus then focused on three areas of normal daily
life. The latter half of chapter 6 (verses 19-34)
gives the warning to the disciples not to depend on
a false sense of security. The key here is anxiety.
Notice the word *worry* in verses 25, 28, 31 and 34.
People of the kingdom were not to worry about
daily provisions.

Bible scholars suggest that quite likely this sermon was given during the Jubilee Year. In his
book, *The Politics of Jesus*,[13] John Howard Yoder
describes what that would have meant for an obedient Jew. You may recall that every seventh year
was a sabbatical year when Jewish people were required to let their fields lie fallow and depend only
on food they could forage. After the seventh sabbatical year, year 49, the Jubilee Year came when

they were again required to leave the fields fallow and undergo radical economic upheaval. Debts were to be forgiven, slaves were to be set free, and land was to be returned to the families of the original owners.

Although this may seem like an unfair economic system to us, it was God's way of reminding His people that He was the owner of all things, and He would rather see that all of the people were taken care of adequately than encourage a self-centered, capitalistic, socially stratified system. If this was a Jubilee Year, then Jesus was calling His followers to obey the Old Testament injunction and depend on God to provide for them. In fact, He was teaching them to take their focus off their immediate earthly concerns and invest in treasures that would not be temporary. Notice in verse 24 the interesting contrast between God and money. Either of them can be a master, and as we give allegiance to one, we neglect the other.

Three particular areas of human life received attention by Jesus, who encouraged His disciples not to worry about food, clothing or the future. Using analogies from nature, Jesus reminded His listeners that even the birds of the air are cared for by the Father who feeds them. Likewise, the vegetation of the earth is clothed in beautiful array, and it is quite unlikely that any lily from the field spends excess time in anxiety. Jesus noted that the pagans are absorbed with issues such as these. Our heavenly Father, however, knows our temporal needs and will supply them if we first seek His kingdom and righteousness. Jesus also insisted that His people are not to be preoccupied about the length of life, since "who of you by worrying can add a single hour to his life" (6:27). An alternate translation reads, "Who of you by worrying can add a single cubit to his height?" In either case, whether it is the measure of one's life or height, worrying adds very little. Jesus said not to worry about tomorrow, assuring that each day has enough trouble of its own.

Next, disciples are warned not to be preoccupied with the faults of others (7:1-14). The human eye is constructed such that it is far easier to see what is external than what is internal. Therefore, as self-appointed moral policemen of the world, human beings are prone to easily see the faults of others and judge them accordingly. Lacking the right perspective causes failure to see one's own faults. The imagery Jesus used here is most humorous. While having a plank in one's own eye, he approaches a brother to try to help him remove the speck of sawdust from his eye.

While a willingness to help others may come from noble motives, Jesus affirmed that disciples may not be qualified to counsel others until they have administered to themselves the same serious introspection and remedial attention. People do not want to be incorrectly judged by those whose own maladies are obvious. In everything the concern ought to be the well-being of others, which is achieved by treating them the way we would want to be treated. Jesus also told His listeners that even when their counsel is good counsel and well-intentioned, it may be rejected (7:6).

Now Jesus' listeners learn that God is a Father who knows how to give good gifts to His children (7:11). Experience with other people may be disillusioning, but Jesus said His children should keep coming to the Father asking, seeking and knocking. In all cases they will find a generous and benevolent Father, who knows their needs and is eager to respond positively. Encouraged by this divine example, disciples can then operate according to the Golden Rule described in verse 12.

Jesus assured His followers that by living according to the Golden Rule, they would be fulfilling the Law and the Prophets. Not many of His contemporaries were living that way, as evidenced by His statement that many people were on the broad way leading to destruction (7:13). Few people enter through the narrow gate, and few travel the narrow road because very few people live out the divine perspective that Jesus has been describing throughout this great sermon.

Finally, Jesus warned His followers to beware of false leaders (7:15-23). Despite what may be favorable outward appearances, such leaders can be identified as false prophets by the fruit of their lives.

Perhaps some might think that here Jesus is contradicting His earlier statement about judging others (7:1). On the contrary, here the topic is wise discernment. This is a kind of judgment that recommends wisdom but excludes condemnation. Many gullible people who do not practice discernment have been led down primrose paths by religiously gifted individuals whose motives are sinister and selfish. Discernment of the lives of leaders is to be based on the fruit of their lives. The metaphors demonstrate this clearly. Grapes do not come from thornbushes, and figs do not grow on thistles.

False leaders have the ability to deceive themselves. Looking toward the future, Jesus anticipated that many would come to Him, seeking entry to the kingdom of heaven based on their spectacular performance. Using their false charisma in prophesying, exorcising, and performing supernatural deeds, they will expect to gain entrance; Jesus, however, affirmed that the only basis for admittance is doing the will of the Father and knowing Him personally (7:21-23). Apart from that relationship, even the so-called good deeds done by such false charismatic leaders are considered to be evil or at least rendered by "evil doers."

A Firm Foundation (Matthew 7:24-29)

This great sermon concludes with an illustration that distinguishes between a wise person and a foolish person. Using the imagery of construction, Jesus noted that the wise person builds his life on a solid foundation so that no matter what dangers and trials assail his life, he will stand firm. That foundation, of course, is the words and teachings of Jesus. Others foolishly neglect the teachings of Jesus and build their life on a foundation of sand rather than rock. When the trials of life come, that person's life will collapse.

In other words, Jesus teaches that the good student is not the one who *learns* the lesson best, but who *lives* the lesson best. The engineer who knows all of the principles of construction, who takes into account all the possible stresses and forces, can still ruin a building if he ignores these principles and builds on the sand. The most ignorant of house builders, however, can rest quite secure, if, even in his ignorance, he builds his structure on the rock. The great teaching found in this Sermon on the Mount is the foundation Jesus sets for His followers. As Paul later stated, "no one can lay any foundation other than the one already laid" (1 Corinthians 3:11).

Endnotes

1. David E. Schroeder, *The Broken God* (Grand Rapids, MI, Baker Books, 1994), p. 115.
2. Ibid., p. 42.
3. Ibid., p. 85.
4. Ibid., p. 27.
5. Ibid., p. 62.
6. Ibid., p. 69.
7. Ibid., p. 16.
8. Ibid., p. 97.
9. John R.W. Stott, *Christian Counterculture*

(Downers Grove, IL: InterVarsity Press, 1978), p. 16.

10. William Barclay, *The Gospel of Matthew*, Vol. 1 (Philadelphia: The Westminster Press, 1958), pp. 124-125.
11. Ibid., p. 125.
12. Ibid., p. 237.
13. John Howard Yoder, *The Politics of Jesus* (Grand Rapids, MI: William B. Eerdmans Publishing Company, 1985), pp. 64ff.

CHAPTER 3

The Kingdom Confronts
The Unclean

Matthew 8-9

For anyone other than the Son of God, delivering a speech as richly inspiring and enlightening as the Sermon on the Mount would have been a great contribution by itself. For Jesus, however, words were never enough. In the second narrative section of his Gospel, Matthew begins to show that Jesus embodied in His life and ministry the very teachings He proclaimed in the Sermon on the Mount.

One of the benefits of Matthew's Gospel, as we have already seen, is its orderly presentation and thematic outline. As we look at the events in this section, the dominant theme is confrontation. Repeatedly, Jesus is brought into contact with elements of society and nature that would ceremonially defile Him according to Jewish scruples. Nevertheless, in each instance we see Jesus in total command, neither fearful of contamination nor cringing from actively imposing the power of the kingdom of God on the problems at hand.

Before examining the episodes of Matthew 8 and 9, we might be helped by employing a mental strategy I often use in trying to gain a clearer understanding of a biblical passage—I try to enter the story and the historical context, not as an observer, but as a participant. Imagine what it might have been like to have heard Jesus preach the Sermon on the Mount. Its impact on us would have been profound. We hear Jesus giving an interpretation of the law that is people-centered. He was moving His disciples away from a legalistic interpretation of Old Testament precepts to a more personal and moral understanding. He was also contrasting true spirituality with false religion.

Many of the sacred disciplines and practices of Judaism, which were considered to be so fundamental to Jewish propriety, were being undermined and replaced by spiritual and attitudinal virtues. Along with the others who heard the sermon, we would have been amazed at His teaching, particularly observing the unique authority with which He spoke. Other rabbis cautiously expounded only on the teachings of previous generations of rabbis. Their sermon manuscripts would be filled with footnotes, whereas Jesus spoke out of His own authority. His authority, however, was noticed not merely in His speaking, but also in His actions. In several of the incidents that follow, it will be the uncontested authority of Jesus that both accomplishes His will and amazes the audience.

Matthew seemed to enjoy reporting about the crowd responses to the authority of Jesus. In chapters 8 and 9, Matthew provides five reports of the crowd's response. In each case we see individuals or crowds who are amazed at the ability of Jesus to control the environment around Him. In 8:27 the disciples are said to marvel because "even the winds and the waves obey him!" In 9:8 after the healing of the paralytic, the multitudes were "filled with awe; and they praised God, who had given such authority to men." Responding to Jesus' giving life back to a little girl, the crowd was so astonished that they spread the news about this miracle throughout the whole land (9:26). After Jesus expelled a demon, the multitudes marveled saying, "Nothing like this has ever been seen in Israel" (9:33). In each of these cases and others that we will see, the unquestionable authority of Jesus stands in the foreground.

Perhaps more amazing than His authority, however, was His own courage in defying the Jewish ceremonial scruples. In an earlier book I have already noted that these two chapters include 12 instances in which Jesus willingly exposed Himself to ceremonially unclean situations. They include: a leper (8:1-4); a Gentile soldier (8:5-13); many demonized people (8:16-17); the sea (8:23-27); tombs, demoniacs and swine (8:28-32); a paralyzed sinner (9:1-6); tax collectors and sinners (9:9-13); a woman with menstrual hemorrhaging

(9:20-22); a corpse (9:23-25); more demons (9:32-
34); and all kinds of diseases and sickness (9:35-
36).[1]

What was the point of all of this? Was Jesus
merely trying to flaunt the conventional wisdom
of His day? Was He a rebel against Jewish propriety and decency? Was His nonconformity a form
of self-promotion? No, Jesus simply knew that effective ministry demands personal involvement.
Sometimes it takes getting dirty to deal with the
dirt, and Jesus did not back down for the sake of
remaining ceremoniously untainted.

Daily Healing Ministry in Capernaum: A Leper (Matthew 8:1-4)

Put yourself in the place of a first-century leper.
Leprosy was among the most terrible of diseases
in the ancient world. Several forms of the dreaded
skin disease could develop, but all of them were
considered to be highly contagious and one of the
greatest horrors of society. The physical decaying
of one's body and the associated stench, pain and
incapacitation might last anywhere from 5 to 30
years. During that time, skin ulcers form and the
body's extremities—fingers, hands, toes and
feet—lose sensation as the muscles waste away.
The tendons contract, leaving clawlike append-
ages until a whole hand or foot might drop off.
The voice becomes reduced to a hoarse wheezing
sound and the leprous person is literally considered to be a walking corpse.

The social trauma of this disease was even

greater. Immediately, when leprosy was diagnosed the leprous person was banished from human society in obedience to Leviticus 13:46, which stated that a leprous person must dwell alone outside of the camp or town. The religious ostracism was just as severe. Of all people in Jewish society, rabbis and priests were the ones who shunned lepers the most.

Matthew 8:2-3 makes two amazing statements. The first is that the leper came to Jesus. After years of being shunned by healthy humans, no leper would dare to approach another person and certainly not a rabbi. The reputation of Jesus must have been such that the leper knew that he would find a welcoming and sympathetic friend in Jesus. The other astonishing statement is that Jesus stretched out His hand and touched the leper. The contagion of leprosy was so great that no one would consider getting closer than six feet to a leper. Nevertheless, Jesus stretched out His hand and touched the leper.

While we admire the leper for his courage, humility and reverence, clearly the spotlight of the passage is on the seeming recklessness of Jesus. Beyond that, however, we stand amazed at His authority. All that Jesus needed to bring healing and life to this walking corpse was the simple statement, "Be clean!"

As if to assure the audience and the leper himself that Jesus was not merely trying to flaunt Judaic scruples by touching a ceremoniously impure person, Jesus then told the healed man to follow the levitical formula of obtaining certification for his cleansing. The process for doing this was somewhat complicated and burdensome, but no doubt Jesus believed it would accomplish two things. First, the man would be reinstated fully into the social and civic life of his community; second, it would assure the Jewish leaders that although Jesus did not always function according to their formulas, He, nevertheless, regarded the Law with greatest respect.

A Soldier's Slave (Matthew 8:5-13)

As astonishing as it was for Jesus to touch a leper, perhaps even more alarming to people of Jewish scruples was His interaction with a Roman centurion. Because Judea was an occupied territory of the Roman Empire, the fiercely independent Jews greatly resented the presence of the Romans. Nevertheless, in most towns, such as Capernaum, there would be at least 100 soldiers under the leadership of a centurion.

The centurion at Capernaum must have been a remarkable man. Luke includes details missing from Matthew's account by mentioning that some of the Jewish elders of Capernaum petitioned Jesus to heal the centurion's servant because, "This man deserves to have you do this, because he loves our nation and has built our synagogue" (Luke 7:4-5). Several facts mentioned in the story reveal the character of the centurion. Not only had he befriended Jewish people and built the synagogue in Capernaum, but he also demonstrated an unusual humaneness among soldiers. In the first century a slave was considered to be a living tool. The Romans said there were three kinds of instruments or tools: the articulate (slaves), the inarticulate (animals) and the mute (vehicles). Not only could slaves be bought and sold, but masters had total power over the life or death of a slave. Thus, it was truly remarkable that a Roman centurion would show such compassion upon a slave.

While the healing of the slave is an important part of the story, certainly the central features of the story are the character of the centurion himself and Jesus' response to him. First notice that Jesus was willing to defile Himself by going to the centurion's house. In Jewish law it was absolutely forbidden for Jews to enter a Gentile's home. Sensitivity to this law probably caused the centurion to tell Jesus not to come under his roof. Then we must also note the centurion's astonishing faith and his view of authority. As a man under authority and as an authority over other men, the centurion understood clearly the principle of authority. He grasped the fact that the sickness of his slave was subject to the authority of the spiritual power of Jesus. Hence, he told Jesus that it would be unnecessary for Him to actually come to heal the servant in person, but merely to give the command for it to be done.

Jesus' reply is the most important part of this story. First, He remarked that He had not found such great faith in anyone in all of Israel. What a slap in the face this was to the Jewish religious leaders, who prided themselves on being people of covenant faith! Jesus pointed to a detestable Gentile soldier and heralded his faith as greater than any in Israel. Furthermore, He asserted that there would be Gentiles at the Messianic banquet. Many others who assumed that they would participate in the feast would be excluded. In fact, they would be cast into outer darkness, the place of weeping and gnashing of teeth.

Second, also notice that Jesus complied with the centurion's request. In fact, He told him to go on his way and that he would find the healing already accomplished. And, sure enough, the text says, "his servant was healed at that very hour" (Matthew 8:13). One of the more subtle points in this story is the fact that Jesus was able to heal from a distance. This has great significance for our day because it is so easy to look back to the first century and say that Jesus' personal presence was the significant factor in His healing of other people. Obviously it was not, because Jesus was able to heal from a distance, just as He is able to do today.

Peter's Mother-in-law and Others (Matthew 8:14-17)

Peter's home in Capernaum was sort of a home away from home for Jesus. After a long day of preaching and healing, Jesus went to Peter's home to spend the night. Arriving there he found an illness in the family. Peter's mother-in-law was lying in bed, suffering from a high fever. Without any great pomp or ceremony, Jesus merely touched her hand, causing the fever to leave.

Mark's account (Mark 1:29-34) tells that this incident occurred on the Sabbath. Later in the evening, after Sabbath was officially over, people who had heard about Jesus' healings and teachings gathered at Peter's home, bringing to Jesus many who were demonized and suffering from other illnesses. Again, without any sensationalism Jesus merely expelled the demons with a word and healed all who were ill. Appealing to Isaiah 53:4, Matthew sees these activities as a fulfillment of Isaiah's prophecy and says, "He took up our infirmities and carried our diseases" (Matthew 8:17).

Going to the Transjordan: Volunteer Disciples (Matthew 8:18-22)

The last half of Matthew 8 shows Jesus moving with His message to the Transjordan area. On the eastern bank of the Sea of Galilee and the Jordan River lived a very mixed population, with Jewish origins but a more syncretistic approach to religion. Being remote to Jerusalem and having Gentile neighbors, the original tribes of Reuben, Gad and half of Manasseh, which chose the eastern bank during the days of Joshua, found it very difficult to be part of the community life of Judaism.

The more chronologically arranged Gospel of Luke showed Jesus giving cross-cultural training prior to sending 70 disciples, two-by-two, to the cities that He was going to visit in the Transjordan area. Matthew's Gospel does not tell us about that mission, but similar instructions are given in chapter 10 to the 12 disciples who were instructed not to go to the Gentiles or the Samaritans, but rather to the lost sheep of the house of Israel. According to Matthew's account, they had already returned from the Transjordan area by this time. But it could well be that the mission of the 12 as well as the mission of the 70 focused on the Transjordan area. The exact chronology and geography of these missions are difficult to discern from the scriptural accounts.

As they were beginning to cross the sea, several individuals approached Jesus. One of them was a scribe who respectfully addressed Jesus as Rabbi and promised that he would follow Jesus anywhere. Jesus responded by saying that whereas foxes and birds have resting places, He Himself lived a more spartan existence. In other words, He was telling the scribe, who may have been accustomed to an easy life, to count the cost. None of the Gospels tell us whether this scribe became a disciple. The second man who came to the Lord wanted first to settle his family matters, including the death and burial of his father. No doubt the father was still alive, and the son, wanting to fulfill traditional domestic obligations, was attempting to delay his discipleship until a more convenient time. On the surface, Jesus' response seems quite harsh: "Let the dead bury their own dead." Yet He knew that if the man did not choose this strategic moment to become a follower, he never would.

Rebuking the Sea (Matthew 8:23-27)

Shortly after entering the boat that was heading for the other side of the sea, Jesus quickly fell into a deep sleep, no doubt exhausted after His previous days of ministry. A fierce storm arose and the boat was taking on water, to the point where the disciples panicked. Perhaps no other event shows as vividly as this the inner serenity of Jesus. He remained asleep in the midst of the storm. The disciples finally woke Him up, yelling, "Lord, save us! We're going to drown!" His response was twofold. First, He reprimanded them for being men of little faith; then He rebuked the winds and the sea, after which it became perfectly calm.

Once again we see Jesus confronting an element with which the rest of Judaism was quite uncomfortable. While it is true that James, John, Peter and Andrew were Jewish fishermen, Jews were generally not fond of the sea. In fact, some even had religious scruples about it. The point of the story being told by Matthew, however, was to show the incredible authority of Jesus, even over nature. The amazement of the disciples at this incident certainly was a step in building their faith.

Tombs, Demons and Swine (Matthew 8:28-34)

Arriving on the east side of the sea, Jesus and the disciples were quickly confronted by two demon-possessed men described as being "so violent that no one could pass that way" (8:28). They lived in a cemetery, constantly crying out and gashing themselves with stones. Upon seeing Jesus, they cried out, "What do you want with us, Son of God? Have you come here to torture us before the appointed time?" Clearly, these demonized men recognized the identity and authority of Jesus.

Again we discover Jesus in a ritually unclean situation. Jews scrupulously avoided any contact with the dead and, therefore, would go great distances out of their way to avoid coming near a cemetery. Also, demons were considered to be the ultimate in defiling a person because of their kinship with Satan. In addition, a herd of pigs was nearby. Obviously, in terms of Jewish purity, Jesus was in a very compromising situation.

The demons certainly knew their time was up and requested that Jesus would cast them into the herd of swine. Obviously they knew the value Jesus placed on human beings and, rather than be banished into the sea, which was considered to be a place of destruction for demons, they opted for the swine. Ultimately, they got both because when they entered into the pigs, the entire herd rushed down the bank into the sea and perished in the water.

The sad sequel to the story is that the herdsman of the pigs went into the city and told about these events, with the result that the people came out to meet Jesus and asked Him to leave their region. In other words, even though the two previously demonized men were restored to sanity and health, the leaders of the city apparently valued pork more than people and asked Jesus—the very One who could bring so much blessing—to leave their region. How sad it is when we value anything more than people, especially the Savior.

Beginnings of Conflict: Healing a Paralyzed Man (Matthew 9:1-8)

Here we find two themes existing side by side. Matthew continues to develop the idea that Jesus was not afraid to confront problems that demanded even that He become ceremonially defiled. But this chapter also begins the drama of conflict with Jewish authorities that would result in His crucifixion. Let us look at this second idea first.

In Matthew 9 we find four accusations being lodged against Jesus. First, in verse 3 some scribes accuse Him of blasphemy because He granted absolution of sins to a paralytic. In verses 10-11 the Pharisees accuse Him of immorality because of His association with tax gatherers and sinners. Then in verses 14-17 we find disciples of John the Baptist accusing Jesus and His followers of slackness in piety because they were not fasting. Finally, in verses 31-34 the Pharisees accuse Jesus of being in an alliance with the devil because He healed a dumb demoniac.

These four accusations are just the beginning of conflict that develops in future chapters. In all of these episodes the clash is between the freedom of Jesus to use His authority redemptively and the fastidiousness of the Jews, particularly the Pharisees, to enforce a standard of piety that emphasized external behavior.

The first of these events occurred in Capernaum after the disciples had returned from their Transjordan mission. Mark's narrative gives more information about the event, stating that four men carried the paralytic to Jesus (Mark 2:3). Not being able to get close enough to Jesus, the enterprising friends of the paralytic brought him to the roof of the lodging and removed some of the pieces of roof to lower the paralytic on his pallet. Seeing the paralyzed man on the bed, Jesus began to minister to him by telling him to take courage because his sins were being forgiven. Hearing this, scribes nearby began to accuse Jesus of blasphemy for claiming to forgive sins. Blasphemy, of course, was a very serious offense in Judaism. Literally, it meant defaming God by reducing His stature in some way. If a person claimed to take upon himself prerogatives of God, such as forgiving sins, surely that would be a blasphemous act. Rather than enter into a theological argument, Jesus chose to exercise His divine authority in a way that would silence His critics.

Undoubtedly, many of those who were present assumed that the paralyzed man was disabled because of sins committed by him or his parents. A reading of John 9:1-3 indicates that the people of this time believed in a direct causal relationship between sin and sickness, a notion that Jesus quickly dispelled there. Here in Matthew 9, however, it seems that the man's paralysis did involve sin. The scribes did not argue with Jesus about the source of the problem, but rather about His seemingly outlandish claim about forgiving the man's sins. The argument Jesus used was a combination of logic and power. He asked them whether it was easier to say your sins are forgiven, or actually to raise the person to full strength and health. Obviously, if the latter could be done, the former was assumed. To the scribes He said, "But so that you may know that the Son of Man has authority on earth to forgive sins . . ." (9:6). Then He concluded His sentence by miraculously raising and healing the paralytic. End of argument. End of discussion.

The crowd of people who witnessed this astonishing miracle were filled with wonder and gave praise to God because He had given such authority to a man. The text does not indicate what the response of the scribes was.

Matthew and Friends (Matthew 9:9-17)

The next episode again shows Jesus' willingness to challenge the religious leaders' erroneous scruples. Tax collectors were among the most hated and disrespected people in Judaism. Because they were employed by the Roman government to collect taxes from the Jewish people and because most of them were professional extortionists, requiring far greater contributions than the law demanded, the Jews despised them and considered them traitors. The man who wrote this Gospel which we are studying was such a man. Matthew was a tax collector. Seeing him at his tax booth, Jesus approached him and said, "Follow me." So, the text says, he "got up and followed him."

Earlier when Jesus had called fishermen to be His disciples, they also left behind their occupations. However, that was not a great sacrifice for fishermen since their social and economic level was relatively low. Matthew, however, was a very prosperous businessman as a tax collector and leaving this post was a great financial sacrifice. Luke's Gospel says that after beginning to follow Jesus, Matthew held a reception in order to honor Jesus and introduce Him to others. Other tax gatherers and sinners were present, as well as some suspicious Pharisees. As protectors of the spiritual purity of Judaism, they became incensed when they saw Jesus eating with tax gatherers and sinners. When Jesus said, "It is not the healthy who need a doctor, but the sick," He was simlpy saying that just as a doctor needs to get close to those who are sick to minister to them, so He needed to be close to sinners to minister to them. Then He challenged the Pharisees to consider the truth of Hosea 6:6, in which God indicates that He prefers compassion and mercy in people to cold-hearted obedience to the laws of sacrifice.

Also at the dinner were disciples of John the Baptist who questioned the laxness of Jesus and His disciples because they did not observe proper Jewish fasting. Perhaps with a bit of self-righteousness in their voice, they asked why they and the Pharisees fasted but the disciples of Jesus refused to do so. Jesus then spoke three parables to correct their understanding.

First, He indicated that fasting was only for a time for those who were mourning. Quite likely the reference to the bridegroom evoked in their memories three passages in Jeremiah (7:34; 16:9; 25:10), which predicted the end of wedding celebrations for brides and bridegrooms during the Babylonian captivity. Later, Jeremiah spoke of the restoration of "the voices of bride and bridegroom" (33:11) once the exiles had returned. This was a pointed way for Jesus to say that Pharisaism was a religion of captivity, whereas His people were disciples of freedom and restoration. The bondage of Pharisaic Judaism was a denial of the kingdom of God. They were still in exile, not in the land of the Lord of liberation.

Verse 15 doubtlessly refers to the time of grief the disciples would experience for three days while Jesus was dead. The phrase "taken from them" suggests a violent removal by death. The reality of His resurrection and abiding presence in the person of the Holy Spirit, however, keeps the disciples of Jesus, the guests of the bridegroom, rejoicing and celebrating. By no means is Christianity simply a "gloom and doom" religion.

The other two parables are equally powerful. While trying to repair an old garment a knowledgeable tailor would not use a patch of new cloth because it has not yet been shrunk. If a new patch were used on an old garment, once the shrinking had taken place, the patch would pull away from the garment and leave another tear. Similarly, Jesus said people do not put unfermented wine into old wineskins because the fermentation of the new wine will force the old wineskins to expand and burst.

What was Jesus suggesting by these parables? The incongruity of the new patch on the old garment and the new wine in the old wineskins shows how Jesus viewed the relationship between His kingdom and Pharisaic Judaism. The two could not possibly mix. Certainly the kingdom could not be sewn onto or be contained by Judaism.

Jesus was saying in a rather enigmatic way that the Pharisees and others would be wrong to use their standards to evaluate Jesus and His followers because the very mission of Jesus was to bring reformation to Judaism in the form of the kingdom of God.

More Astonishing Healings (Matthew 9:18-38)

Interrupting this dinner party was a synagogue official who came and bowed before Jesus announcing that his daughter had just died. The official was confident, however, that if Jesus would come and lay His hand upon her, she would live. While making their trek to the home of Jairus, as he is called by Mark and Luke, Jesus was approached by a woman who secretly came up behind Him and touched the fringe of His cloak. In her own simple way she believed that if only she could touch the cloak of Jesus, she would be made well after suffering for 12 years from an uncontrollable hemorrhage. Mark and Luke give us much more detail than does Matthew. In the midst of a jostling crowd, Jesus stopped and asked who had touched Him. In astonishment, the disciples reminded Jesus that many people were touching Him. But Jesus kept looking until He finally identified the woman, who fearfully admitted that she was the one who had touched Him. Rather than scolding her, Jesus affirmed her courage and faith. Then she was healed.

The woman's hemorrhaging for 12 years was undoubtedly an unstoppable flow of menstrual blood. In their fastidiousness about cleanliness the Jews had an abundance of regulations and prohibitions having to do with the contamination of menstrual blood. Suffice it to say here that during the time of her period, a woman was ostracized from the rest of the community. Thus for 12 years this woman had been every bit as much an outcast as a leper.

Obviously she had seen something in Jesus that gave her the courage to violate the Jewish scruple by touching His garment. Any other rabbi in the same situation would have been incensed with so-called righteous indignation. Jesus, however, responded in gentleness and mercy.

Arriving at the home of Jairus, Jesus and His disciples found quite a scene. The flute players and professional mourners were already wailing and mourning and creating a typical scene of great grief. With His customary authority, Jesus told

these people to leave the house and indicated that
the little girl was merely asleep. Knowing for a
fact that she was dead, the people began laughing
at Jesus. Nevertheless, after putting them out of
the house, He then went in, took the girl by the
hand and raised her up to new life. Mark indicates
that immediately the girl arose and began to walk.
Everyone who was there, including the disciples
and parents, was utterly amazed. Even though Jesus gave them strict orders not to report this
(Mark 5:43), Matthew indicates that "news of this
spread through all that region" (Matthew 9:26).

Other miracles followed. As Jesus was traveling
with His disciples one day, two blind men heard
that He was passing by and started following, crying out, "Have mercy on us, Son of David" (9:27).
When they arrived at their destination and had
gone indoors, presumably to be out of public
view, Jesus asked the blind men whether they believed He was able to restore their sight. When
they indicated their faith in Him, He touched
their eyes and said, "According to your faith will
it be done to you" (9:29). The text simply says,
"and their sight was restored" (9:30).

Not wanting His fame to spread, Jesus
warned them not to tell others about this
astonishing healing; nevertheless, they went out
and spread the news about Him throughout the
region.

The last healing in this chain of miracles was a
dumb man who was demonized. Other people
brought this man to Jesus, who expelled the de-

mon and enabled the dumb man to speak. The multitudes marveled saying, "Nothing like this has ever been seen in Israel" (9:33). The crowd reacted with wonder and amazement. The Pharisees responded by cynically suggesting that the power of Jesus to expel demons had come from union with Satan, the ruler of the demons.

As we come to the end of these busy days of Jesus' life in which He touched so many people in miraculous ways, we are amazed at His energy, His compassion, His willingness to interact with social and spiritual outcasts, His reluctance to achieve notoriety and His absolute authority over every element of humanity and nature. No wonder the text keeps saying that the news about Him continued to spread throughout the land.

Despite all of these healings, the real heart of Jesus is seen in verses 35 to 36; He continued traveling through the cities and villages teaching in the synagogues about the gospel of the kingdom. Although He continued to heal people of many types of diseases, He focused primarily on the individuals who so desperately needed the salvation that He could bring. Verse 36 is especially poignant: "When he saw the crowds, he had compassion on them, because they were harassed and helpless, like sheep without a shepherd." What good news it was for all of Israel that at last a Shepherd had come, a Shepherd who would risk everything to save His sheep.

Endnotes

1. David E. Schroeder, *"Follow Me"*: *The Master's Plan for Men* (Grand Rapids: Baker Book House, 1992), p. 200.

CHAPTER 4

Service in the Kingdom

Matthew 10

In the previous section we saw Jesus confronting unclean elements of society by invoking the power of the new kingdom He was introducing. He cleansed a leper (Matthew 8:3), expelled many unclean spirits (8:16), expelled some exceedingly violent demons (8:32) and healed a paralytic (9:6). Chapter 9 ended with Jesus calling His disciples to work in the harvest field that He said was already ripe and needing many workers. Chapter 10 begins with Jesus summoning His 12 disciples and giving them the same authority that He exercised to heal people of their diseases and to cast out unclean spirits. The ones He imbued with this special authority seemed to have been relatively unknown and normal men. What set them apart from others was that Jesus specifically chose them for this apostolic ministry. They were to be His agents for introducing the message and power of the kingdom.

We can be encouraged that Jesus is not looking merely for people with high credentials but people who are available to serve Him and through whom He can exercise His power. William Barclay says, "Jesus is looking for ordinary men who can do ordinary things extraordinarily well." But we can only do things extraordinarily well when we are equipped with the power that Jesus gives us.

The reason Jesus was so eager to multiply His ministry through others goes back to a comment that appears in Matthew 9:35. Notice that Jesus was going through the cities and villages teaching in the synagogues, proclaiming the gospel of the kingdom and healing all kinds of diseases and sicknesses. Why was He doing this? Because, as verse 36 mentions, He felt compassion for them. The people were distressed and beaten down like sheep without a shepherd. The Greek word for "compassion" refers to feeling something at the "gut level." The idea is that Jesus felt the plight of His people so keenly that He became physically agitated in the center of His being. This great compassion motivated Jesus to multiply His ministry through His disciples.

If you are a student of the Gospels, you already know that not all four Gospel writers present all the same details of the life of Jesus. Taken as a whole, all four Gospels present a fairly full story, we suspect. Our understanding of the preparation of the 12 for ministry is amplified greatly by Mark's Gospel, where 3:13-6:7 gives information not included by Matthew. In other words, we see that Jesus chose the 12 and then ministered to them and with them for a period of time before actually sending them out on their own mission.

The Twelve (Matthew 10:1-4)

Although we know little about them, the 12 He chose seem to be a curious lot. Two of them, namely, Peter and John, have character sketches drawn out fairly well in Scripture. We also know James, Philip, Thomas and Nathaniel fairly well. Judas we know primarily because of his infamy. The rest we know only by name. People have tried to piece together profiles of these disciples by using tradition. Alfred Plummer says, "The traditions about them are very untrustworthy, and perhaps are mere conjectures, framed to mask unwelcome ignorance."[1] He also notes that "in the New Testament it is the work and not the workers that is glorified."[2] In one sense, their day is yet to come. Revelation 21:14 says the walls of the heavenly city will have 12 foundation stones, each with the name of one of the apostles. Apparently these are parallel to the gates of 12 angels in which are etched the names of the 12 tribes of the sons of Israel. If we wonder why Jesus chose specifically 12 apostles, perhaps He had in mind this parallel with the 12 sons of Israel.

Because of the dramatic way in which the story of Jesus' life ends, we may pause here for a moment to note the notorious Judas Iscariot, the last of the 12 to be listed. Other than being the last name mentioned, there is no hint that Judas was in any way different from the other 11. He was one who went on the mission in Matthew 10. Like the others, he returned apparently after having ministered successfully. The call of Jesus, while giving special authority, did not exempt any of the 12 from the possibility of being faithless if they so willed. And in time Judas came to that point. Plummer says of Judas, "His treachery is proof that no office in the Church, however exalted, gives security: disastrous downfall is possible even for those who have been nearest to Christ."[3] We will have more to say about Judas as we proceed toward the end of Matthew's Gospel.

Instructions for the Mission (Matthew 10:5-15)

The first instruction Jesus gave the 12 may seem quite odd and somewhat offensive. He told them not to go to the Gentiles or the Samaritans. This is consistent with His concern that the Jews be given the first opportunity to hear the gospel. His last instruction to them (Acts 1:8) gave an order of priority: Jerusalem, Judea, Samaria and then the remotest part of the earth. There were several reasons for this instruction. First, several Old Testament passages (for example, Genesis 12:3; Exodus 19:6; Psalm 2:8; Isaiah 9:1-2; Isaiah 49:6; Jonah 4:11) indicate that God raised up Israel to be a priest to the other nations who would also become part of God's kingdom. By taking the message of the kingdom first to the Jews, Jesus was deliberately preparing the nation of priests so that their ministry to the Gentiles could be full. Second, up to this point the disciples had no experience in cross-cultural ministry. As typical Jews of their day, their cultural experience was homogeneous. Not only did their religious scruples separate them from the Gentiles, but their understanding of the Gentile mind was also quite limited. Barclay notes, "Before the gospel could effectively be brought to the Gentiles, a man with Paul's life and background had to emerge."[4] A further reason for this limited ministry was simply that with such a small force of workers it was eminently practical to concentrate the ministry on a rather small area. Only when Galilee was successfully evangelized with the gospel would Jesus have an adequate foundation for pursuing other areas. As we know from the subsequent story, the gospel eventually spread into Samaria and Judea on the south, Decapolis on the east and Syria on the north. And then after the earthly life of Jesus, the apostles continued to take the gospel further to the south in North Africa, to the east all the way to India and perhaps China and to the north and west into Asia Minor, Greece and Europe.

Perhaps there is a practical word in this limitation of ministry given by Jesus. In essence it suggests to us that if we can't do it at home we have no business trying to export it. This is why many mission boards require a period of effective home service before allowing missionary candidates to go overseas.

Matthew 10:6 offers another insight into the

psyche of Jesus. His instruction to the disciples was to go to "the lost sheep of Israel." We have already seen that Jesus had great compassion on the multitudes because they were like sheep without a shepherd (9:36). The special compassion Jesus had for His people Israel suggests that despite the future overwhelming success of the gospel among the Gentiles, Jesus never meant for Christianity to be a Gentile religion. Perhaps the greatest tragedy in the history of God's eternal plan is that Christianity is so exclusively associated with the Gentile world. How thrilling it is today when we meet a Messianic Jew, a person born of Jewish descent who embraces Jesus as Messiah.

The instructions Jesus gave the 12 are quite specific and perhaps a bit unusual. Their mission was to be both in word and deed, in proclamation and power, in declaration and demonstration, in message and ministry. Specifically, they were to go with the message, "The kingdom of heaven is at hand." Because Matthew's Gospel is often called the Gospel of the kingdom, and because this sermon theme is so important, let us pause to explore what Jesus meant when He referred to the kingdom of God.

> A few statements about the nature of the kingdom must be made to counteract some of the erroneous notions of our day. The kingdom of God for Jesus did not mean heaven, although heaven certainly will be the fullest expression of the kingdom of

God. The kingdom of God for Jesus meant the rule of God in the hearts and lives of people who know, love, and obey God. Thus it is a reign, not a realm. It is not a place where Jesus owns protectorship and government control. It is an active power in people due to the authority of God in their lives. The kingdom of God is "realized but not yet." This is a phrase used by theologians to show the double dimension of the kingdom. It is very much like an embryo growing in a womb. It is there, it is alive, it is growing, but it has not been given birth. It is both here and now as well as then and there.[5]

Certainly, a kingdom of this nature could not adequately be described by mere preaching. Jesus instructed His disciples to use His authority to heal the sick, raise the dead, cleanse the lepers and cast out demons. Such impressive displays of power would certainly capture the attention of the people. In fact, well into the apostolic era, as we see in the book of Acts, signs and wonders continued to play an important role in evangelism. In our generation we have seen an active discussion about "signs and wonders" theology. Viewpoints on the issue go from one extreme to the other. On the one hand, dispensationalists emphasize that this authority was given only to the 12 apostles, and once they were gone the church had to rely on the power of the Spirit of God to use the written Word of God to convince people about the reality of Jesus. On the other hand, a school of thought represented by people like John Wimber believes that the power to perform signs and wonders is still available to the church today and that God intends for believers to exercise the authority of Jesus in supernatural ways to convince the world of the truth of Christianity.

Both viewpoints seem to be contradicted by our experience. While modern Christians do not seem to have quite the same ability as the apostles in exercising signs and wonders, surely God has acted frequently in supernatural ways throughout church history to demonstrate His power. People continue to be healed and the Spirit of God continues to work miraculously through the church. On the other hand, even those who espouse the signs and wonders theology haven't exactly captured the world's attention by sustained and predictable performance of miracles. God seems to have placed some degree of limitation on the authority He has given to modern disciples. Perhaps the following ideas presented in one of my earlier books may be helpful here.

> The occurrence of a miracle was considered by the Jews to be a sign that God was sanctioning the activity of the agent of the miracle. Thus, Jesus used miracles in the promotion of his spiritual kingdom. When He left earth only a small body of inconsequential Jews believed that He still lived and

that the kingdom would proceed. The best "proof" of His resurrection, the best apologetic to convince the Jews of Jesus' Messiahship had to be the continuation of the miracles in his name. This was not to be a substitute for saving faith but a catalyst for it. These having been done and recorded historically, no need remained for this type of miracle. Hence, the disappearance of them in Acts. This is not to rule out miracles today, but to show a distinction in purpose and thereby the present infrequency. They were done almost indiscriminately in Acts as an apologetic. They are done very discriminately today as sheer grace. The individual, not the kingdom as such, is the focus of today's miracles.[6]

After giving the primary instructions to preach and heal, Jesus gave some secondary instructions in verses 9-15. Essentially, the disciples were told not to seek to profit financially by their ministry, but were told to accept the support and hospitality of the people to whom they ministered. They were told to travel lightly and to seek to bring and be a blessing wherever they went. On the other hand, when they were not welcomed, they were not to remain in those places that withheld hospitality, but were merely to "shake the dust off your feet" in protest against that house or city. Notice here that Jesus was instructing His followers not to try to argue anyone into the kingdom. Instead,

He wanted them merely to announce the presence of the kingdom and keep moving on with the message. Those cities that refused the message about the kingdom, unfortunately, would suffer more than the dust from the shoes of the disciples. Jesus said that the cities of Sodom and Gomorrah had it easier than these cities in the judgment day. Throughout Scripture the cities of Sodom and Gomorrah represent exceeding wickedness (see Matthew 11:23-24; Luke 10:12-13; 17:29; Romans 9:29; 2 Peter 2:6; Jude 7). Sodom and Gomorrah were decisively judged by God not only for their exceeding immorality and wickedness, but also for their lack of hospitality to the people and message of God. Similarly, cities that blatantly rejected the announcement of the coming kingdom would experience harsh judgment.

Warnings about Persecution (Matthew 10:16-23)

Jesus was well aware that the mission He was sending His disciples on would be dangerous. They were going, He said, as sheep into a pack of wolves. Why would anyone send sheep into a pack of wolves?

Jesus sent His disciples as sheep into the pack of wolves in order to rescue the other sheep (9:36). But He told them not to be like typical sheep. They were to be "shrewd as snakes and as innocent as doves" (10:16). Those familiar with sheep know that they could be described as innocent, but certainly not shrewd. Verses 17-20 describe the shrewdness that Jesus had in mind. The disciples were to be aware of the tactics of their enemies. They would be persecuted by the courts, the synagogues and their own family members.

In our day we would say that we can expect to be harassed by the state, the church and our families. The transparent honesty of Jesus is remarkable here. We might think that these comments would have discouraged even the hardiest of soldiers. Nevertheless, Jesus wanted His disciples to know that the message about the kingdom would be so controversial and alarming that they would be brought before governors and kings which, in fact, we see taking place in the book of Acts. Jesus promised that when the disciples did appear before authorities to explain why they were causing trouble by delivering such a strange message, they need not be anxious about how they would respond. They would know what to say at that time by the power of the Spirit of God who would speak through them.

Verse 19 and its parallel verses in Luke 21:14-15 need to be understood in their context. People have abused these verses by claiming that they never need to prepare in advance for ministry. Even preachers have used these verses to excuse their lack of careful preparation of sermons, assuming that these verses promise that the Spirit of God will speak through them even if they do not prepare in advance. Actually, the promise refers to the specific situation where the disciple is called before a public court to give defense of his ministry. In that situation, the disciples need not be anxious because God wants to use them as "witnesses to them and to the Gentiles" (Matthew 10:18).

Verse 21 is an especially difficult verse to handle in our day because of the strong emphasis on building family values. Here and in other places Jesus emphasized that the kingdom of God and its urgency make even family relationships secondary (see also Matthew 10:35-37; Luke 9:59-60). Obviously, Jesus was not recommending to His disciples that they act in a way that would elicit hostility from their family. However, surely He wanted the disciples to proclaim and demonstrate the kingdom, even to family members. Inevitably, some family members would hate the disciples of Jesus because of the message. In such an instance, the disciple must still hold firm in being faithful to his ministry. Even when disciples would be put to death, which would occur frequently in the days of the early church, they could be assured that because they endured to the end, they would be saved (Matthew 10:22).

As we read this section of instructions, we are impressed with the total honesty of Jesus. He told the disciples that although they would be rejected, ostracized, hated and persecuted, they still needed to keep moving with the message. He clearly told them their task in the grimmest possible terms. Plummer notes, "That is not the world's way of winning adherents."[7] Modern church growth theory has no parallel to this tactic. Today we emphasize "user-friendly discipleship." And often it is suggested that the primary motive for being a disciple of Jesus is to experience self-fulfillment. The early disciples might have scratched their heads a few times about the clever way we are able to glamorize the call to ministry. History, however, proves that the method of Jesus had been right. The great saying, "The blood of the martyrs is the seed of the church," is a truth we cannot dispel. Wherever the church has thrived, disciples have suffered.

Encouragement about Discipleship (Matthew 10:24-33)

Having explained the mission and the methodology they were to use, and having warned the disciples that they would experience great resistance to the message, Jesus then gave the disciples some encouragement. This encouragement might seem very comforting for the disciples to know that they were being privileged to experience the same rejection that Jesus would experience. In a day when we are so allergic to rejection, we may have a hard time identifying with the disciples and especially with the apostle Paul, who said that part of his motivating goal was to participate in "the fellowship of sharing in his sufferings, becoming like him in his death" (Philippians 3:10). Presumably the bond between Jesus and His disciples was so great that they would consider it a high privilege to be treated in the same way as their master. They were members of His household

(Matthew 10:25) and that honor was more than
enough comfort to offset the pain of rejection.

We have entitled this section "Encouragement
about Discipleship" because we see Jesus trying to
instill courage in the disciples. Three times He
tells them not to fear. In verse 26, they are not to
fear because truth will triumph. In verse 28, they
are not to fear because they will survive death.
And in verse 31, they are not to fear because God
values them greatly. In other places Jesus tells the
disciples not to be anxious about anything but to
go boldly forward in ministry despite all the opposition and the odds.

Why did Jesus focus so much on anxiety and
fear? Without any doubt, fears are primarily what
immobilize and paralyze people from positive living and ministry. No one who was afraid to take a
risk ever accomplished anything great for God. In
fact, one scholar has noted that every time where
great advances are gained for the people of God in
both Old Testament and New Testament, two
conditions prevail; prayer and taking a risk. Often
today we hear people of God called to prayer. But
how often do we hear people challenged to take a
risk? Jesus was clearly calling His disciples to take
risks for the advancement of the kingdom. And in
taking risks they were not to fear.

Verse 27 is repeated frequently in the Gospels.
Mark 4:22, Luke 8:17 and Luke 12:2 are quite
similar to Matthew 10:27. In fact, the present
verse seems to shed light on the other three. For
example, Luke 12:2 says, "There is nothing con-

cealed that will not be disclosed, or hidden that will not be made known." The idea is that the great news about the kingdom, the gospel of Jesus Christ, could not be contained or held secret. The message is so illuminating that it will come to light. Certainly it should not be put under a bushel, but on a lamp stand (Mark 4:21-22).

Notice the radical saying in Luke 12:2—"There is nothing concealed that will not be disclosed, or hidden that will not be made known." What did Jesus mean by this saying? We might at first be inclined to interpret it eschatologically, that is, to assume Jesus was warning His followers that every word they say will be made known publicly in the time of judgment, so they had better be careful about their speech. Perhaps our confusion about this verse arises because the same idea and words are found in three other New Testament passages: Matthew 10:26 parallels [the] text, Luke 12:2, but the next verse is worded differently. In the Matthew version, Jesus clearly instructs His disciples to speak in daylight what He told them in the dark, and to proclaim from rooftops what He whispered in their ear. They should not be afraid of the consequences. Although they might be killed for their honest discipleship, this would be preferable to being disowned by the Father in heaven because they had concealed what Jesus had taught them.[8]

The second reason for not fearing is that the disciples of Jesus are spiritually immortal. Yes, someone may kill their body, but no one is able to kill the soul. The disciples are instructed to fear Him who is able to destroy both the soul and the body in hell. We understand that here Jesus was referring to a healthy fear of God who alone has control over a person's destiny. The author of Hebrews suggests a similar idea: "It is a dreadful thing to fall into the hands of the living God" (Hebrews 10:31).

In Matthew 10:28 "hell" translates a Greek word translated elsewhere as Gehenna, which also referred to the Valley of Hinnom located south of Jerusalem. This valley had a notorious history as a place for idol worship (1 Kings 11:7) and the sacrificing of children (2 Chronicles 28:3). Jeremiah predicted that it would become the Valley of Slaughter (Jeremiah 7:31-32). In Jesus' time this valley was the city dump. Like most city dumps, it smoldered constantly, emitted a putrid odor and was infested with detestable creatures. Accordingly, it became an apt metaphor for the concept of eternal destruction. Unlike the Greek concept of Hades, which referred to a shadowy world of perpetual disembodied existence, Gehenna suggested a place of conscious torment for those who resisted God's love and grace.

The Valley of Gehenna was an apt metaphor for hell for another reason, too. The residents of

Jerusalem used it as a dump to dispose of their rubbish because it was useless to them. Likewise, God will dispose of humans, not primarily because He is angry with them but because of their uselessness to Him. We understand from Scripture that God has created humans to "love Him and enjoy Him forever." This can be done only by those who have experienced His forgiving grace. If we are designed to be eternal worshipers of almighty God, only those who have received His Spirit have an eternal function. All others are useless to God and, therefore, will experience Gehenna eternally. C.S. Lewis suggests that hell will be the only comfortable place for non-worshipers because God is everywhere else.[9]

Jesus, however, encourages the disciples to know that each of them is of infinite and eternal value to the heavenly Father (Matthew 10:29-31). Even little sparrows, being of little commercial value, are carefully watched and cared for by the Father. The disciples are told that God knows even how many hairs are on their heads. So great is the Father's knowledge and awareness of His children! This is the third reason why the disciples are told not to fear. Their value is very great in the eyes of the heavenly Father.

The Cost of Discipleship (Matthew 10:34-42)

Having given words to encourage the disciples, Jesus then turned His attention again to some of the realities of discipleship. While the gospel certainly brings peace to the human soul by reconciling the sinner to God and breaking down the spiritual wall that separates us from our Father, the gospel does not bring peace to the earth. Jesus could not have said it more plainly than in Matthew 10:34. His purpose never was political. Jesus came not as the bearer of prosperity or peace. He came not to win popularity; rather, His coming has set family members against one another, and has made disciples the enemies of members of their own family (Matthew 10:35-36). Using a quotation from Micah 7:6, Jesus described how families would be separated because of the gospel.

This is not an easy passage to deal with in our day. The disintegration of the family due to all kinds of social problems has rightly caused the Christian church to emphasize family values and the importance of Christian families as strong witnesses in our society. Obviously, Jesus was not encouraging His disciples to create hostility in their families. If the verses here sound as though Jesus deliberately was setting His disciples against their family members, perhaps we misunderstand the verses. Rather, Jesus was merely predicting that His coming to earth to establish the kingdom of God would cause separations within families. Even today in many Middle Eastern and Oriental societies a person who embraces Jesus as Messiah and Savior may be ostracized from his or her family. Jesus' prediction was correct.

Far from devaluing the importance of the family, Jesus specifically used the family concept to show just how important and all embracing is the call to the kingdom. It transcends even the natural bond of human families. If Jesus wanted to communicate the infinite priority of the kingdom over human relationships, He could not have chosen a more highly honored or valued institution than the family. In comparison to the natural claim of family members to be loyal and faithful to one another, the claim of the kingdom upon an individual is far greater. That is why Jesus said, "Anyone who loves his father or mother more than me is not worthy of me; anyone who loves his son or daughter more than me is not worthy of me" (Matthew 10:37).

To be sure, the call to the kingdom, while being a powerful and positive call to join the purposes and program of God, is also a call that requires sacrifice. Verses 38-39 give the essence of discipleship.

> Self-denial means ego transference, subordinating my sense of independence and me-ism to the cause of Christ. . . . Often we define our cross as any burden that we are called on to bear . . . that was not what He meant when He said, "Take up your cross." A cross is a device that will kill you, a symbol of total sacrifice. . . . The cross is where you find death to self.[10]

William Barclay comments,

> There is no place for a policy of safety first

in the Christian life. The man who seeks
first ease and comfort and security and the
fulfillment of personal ambition may well
get all these things but he will not be a
happy man. For he was sent into this world
to serve God and to serve his fellow men. A
man can hoard life if he wishes to do so but
that way he will lose all that makes life valuable to others and worth living to himself.
The way to serve others, the way to fulfill
God's purposes for us, the way to true happiness is to spend life, for only then will we
find life here and hereafter.[11]

Referring to the phrase, "for my sake" in verse
39, Alfred Plummer notes that here

we have a claim which is monstrous if He
who makes it is not conscious of being Divine, Who is it that is going to own us or re-
nounce us before God's judgment-seat
(32-33)? Who is it that promises with such
confidence that the man who loses his life
for his sake shall find it? And these momen-
tous utterances are spoken as if the Speaker
had no shadow of doubt as to their truth,
and as if He expected that His hearers
would at once accept them.[12]

Certainly anyone who uttered these ideas
would be considered the height of arrogance if He
were not truly the Son of God. Only the Savior

who self-consciously was calling into existence a kingdom that was part and parcel of the eternal plan of God could utter this statement of expectation for His disciples. Plummer continues, "What is more, thousands of Christians, generation after generation, have shaped their lives by them and have proved their truth by repeated experience."[13]

Because of their intimate identification with the person of Jesus, the disciples would be His immediate representatives, regardless of where they ministered. That is why people who received them would actually be credited as receiving Jesus, and also receiving God the Father. Jesus continued the thought of how the disciples would be received by promising that they would be going forth as prophets so that when they were received as prophets and as righteous men, those who received them would indeed be honored by God. But as great as their mission was and their rank as apostles and prophets was, the disciples ultimately needed to remember that they were still weak and vulnerable. Indeed, they were like little children who would go forth needing even the most basic of supplies such as cold water. Again, the people who ministered to the disciples, whether as prophets, as righteous men or even as disciples, would not lose their reward (10:42).

Today's Relevance

This second discourse of Jesus in the Gospel of Matthew was addressed specifically to the disciples in preparation for their ministry in Galilee. The

four sections we have studied above contain many
difficult verses. Some of them we would just as
soon ignore, but we would do so at our peril. The
extreme relevance of this chapter for modern Christian ministry is evident in the following ideas:

1. Verses 5-15 teach us that effective ministry for
   the kingdom needs to be a combination of effective proclamation and powerful demonstration.
   Both words and deeds must communicate the
   nature of the gospel. The distinction between
   evangelism and the so-called social gospel must
   diminish so that all ministry comes from both
   the heart and the hand.

2. Verses 16-23 warn us to be prepared for persecution. Whenever the gospel has successfully
   penetrated a culture, some of the communica-
   tors of the gospel have been greatly abused.
   This world has never been a friend to grace
   and those who bring the gospel of peace are
   often those who suffer the most.

3. Verses 24-33 encourage us to keep focused on
   eternal consequences, knowing what the end
   result is for obedience, and conversely, the end
   result for disobedience. Ministry is risky but
   Jesus encourages His disciples not to fear anyone but almighty God. The disciple of Jesus
   has diplomatic immunity as he carries the
   message of the king into the alien territories of
   earthly culture.

4. And finally, verses 34-42 teach that our relationships and values need to be radically pro-kingdom. We may even need to replace our closest and most intimate earthly associations with relationships to Jesus and His people.

Endnotes

1. Alfred Plummer, *An Exegetical Commentary on The Gospel of St. Matthew* (Grand Rapids: Baker Book House, 1982), p. 146.
2. Ibid.
3. Ibid., p. 148.
4. William Barclay, *The Gospel of Matthew*, Vol. 1 (Philadelphia: The Westminster Press, 1958), p. 373.
5. David E. Schroeder, *Follow Me Manual* (Laguna Niguel, CA: MasterWorks, Inc, 1992).
6. David E. Schroeder, *"Follow Me"* (Grand Rapids: Baker Book House, 1992), p. 130.
7. Plummer, p. 152.
8. *Follow Me*, pp. 163-164.
9. C.S. Lewis, "The Trouble with X," in *God in the Dock* (Grand Rapids, MI: William B. Eerdmans, 1970), pp. 154-155. Se also in the same volume Lewis' article, "The Humanitarian Theory of Punishment."
10. *Follow Me*, pp. 163-164.
11. Barclay, p. 409.
12. Plummer, p. 157.
13. Ibid.

CHAPTER 5

Opposition to the Kingdom

Matthew 11-12

In the last section we saw that Jesus anticipated a road strewn with conflict and danger for Himself and His followers. In Matthew 10:25, He anticipated that both He and they would be called "Beelzebub." The disciples did not have to wait long before the conflict ensued. In this section we find the Pharisees accusing Jesus of casting out demons by "Beelzebub" (12:24). In fact, chapters 11 and 12, the next narrative section, consist mostly of the growing hostility against Jesus and the increasing opposition to the kingdom.

Matthew 11:1 gives an "end of discourse" formula, the one we have already seen. The NASB gives a close translation by saying, "And it came about that when Jesus had given instructions. . . ." Chapter 11 seems to be mostly discourse but we will see that the words of Jesus are in response to activities occurring as He and the disciples encounter events and people. Chapter 12 consists entirely of conflict with the Pharisees. All five of the discourses in Matthew end with a form of the Greek verb *teleo*, which means to bring to an end, finish or complete something. In each case the goal achieved is the completion of a discourse narrative.

Sayings about John the Baptist (Matthew 11:1-19)

Even if Jesus had never come, there can be no question that John the Baptist would still have been a very imposing figure in Jewish history. His was the first prophetic voice in 400 years to move the Jewish people toward repentance. Many were thinking that he would be God's Messiah. Nevertheless, John steadfastly refused that role, but insisted that his task was to prepare the way for the coming Messiah. As a man of unbending conviction and unfettered courage, John readily raised the ire of the political and religious authorities. Thus, as Matthew 11 opens, we find John in prison having some very understandable second thoughts about his life and ministry—and particularly, the role of Jesus. Being an aggressive and energetic man, John was probably not the best candidate for living in prison peaceably. Alfred Plummer comments that at this time John's patience, not his faith, was wavering. He sent his disciples to find out whether or not Jesus was going to start acting like the Messiah, as John assumed the Messiah should act. His question, "should we expect someone else?" may well have been a sarcastic way of telling Jesus to get on with His mission.[1]

The reply of Jesus was a simple lesson about the Messiah. Quoting from Isaiah 61, Jesus indicated to John through his disciples that miracles of mercy were being wrought, giving testimony to the fulfillment of God's purposes through the Messiah: The blind receive sight, the lame walk, the lepers are cleansed, the deaf hear, the dead are raised up, and the poor have the gospel preached to them.

Let us notice at this point the wonderful integration of ministry in the life of Jesus between words and action. He told the disciples of John to go tell John what they were seeing and what they were hearing. The authoritative message of Jesus was not only instructional, it was transformational. But notice also the priority of Jesus. The last phrase, "the good news is preached to the poor," is somewhat of a surprise. In the previous four illustrations, the resulting action totally relieves the sufferer: Blind people begin to see, lame people walk, lepers are healed, and the deaf hear. We might expect that the response of Jesus to the poor would be to give them money to relieve them of their poverty. Not so. Apparently what the poor need more than anything is the preaching of the gospel. This should not be used as an excuse for Christians to shirk social responsibility; rather, it is merely a statement of priority.

The last comment of Jesus to the disciples of John was, "Blessed is the man who does not fall

away on account of me" (Matthew 11:6). Jesus
was warning John not to take offense even though
he was tempted to stumble.

As the disciples of John were leaving to bring
the message of Jesus to the prophet/prisoner, Jesus
began to pay a great tribute to John by speaking to
the multitudes. He asked a series of questions to
affirm the lofty role of John the Baptist. First, He
asked what the people expected when they went
out to the wilderness. Did they expect to see a
weak reed being blown about by the wind? What
did they expect to see? Someone who was arrayed
in luxurious clothing? He then followed these rhetorical questions by asking a third time, "What did
you go out to see?" Then He asked, "A prophet?
Yes, I tell you, and more than a prophet" (11:9).
Jesus then quoted Malachi 3:1 to reveal John's
identity: "I will send my messenger ahead of you,
who will prepare your way before you." John understood his role. Jesus understood the role of
John. And Jesus wanted the people to have a right
understanding of John's identity.

Without any doubt, by identifying John as the
forerunner to the Messiah, Jesus was also strongly
affirming to the people that He Himself was the
Messiah being introduced by John. We have already seen in Matthew 3 that Jesus, rather shock-
ingly, submitted to the baptism of John to identify
with the ministry and message of John. In many
ways Jesus and John were linked together in the
minds of the people. Those who were prone to accept John would likely accept Jesus; those who re-

jected John would likely reject Jesus.

Verse 11 indicates the great respect Jesus had for John. Jesus stated that among those born of women, John the Baptist was the greatest. Jesus qualified that by saying, "Yet he who is least in the kingdom of heaven is greater than he." That may seem to be confusing, but if we connect this idea with Matthew 9:15, we may come to a better understanding. Responding to the inquiry of John's disciples regarding fasting, Jesus used an analogy in which He compared Himself to the bridegroom and John to the best man or the friend of the bridegroom. The qualitative difference is the same as that between members of the kingdom of God, or the kingdom of heaven, and those who are not yet part of that kingdom.

If verse 11 is difficult to understand, verse 12 is truly an enigma, and one which has evoked thousands of paragraphs by commentators. What does it mean to assert that from the days of John the Baptist up until the moment of this statement that the kingdom of heaven was forcefully advancing, and forceful men were taking hold of it? And what relationship does that have with the following verses that talk about the law and the prophets preceding John, and John himself fulfilling the prophetic role of Elijah? The question is worth pondering, but perhaps impossible to answer conclusively. Luke 16:16 presents the same ideas, but indicates a greater finality to the role of the law and the prophets and a break between their ministry and the proclamation of the good news of the

kingdom of God. When John began announcing
the coming of the kingdom, people responded to
his preaching with violent or forceful reactions, as
they began thronging both John and Jesus. We
have already seen in Matthew 3:5 that people from
Jerusalem, Judea and all the district around the
Jordan were going out to be baptized by John. In
other words, the ministry of John was like a great
shock wave within Judaism, and people were pan-
icking in their eagerness to confess their sins and
be baptized by John. It was an apocalyptic moment for sure. And Jesus did not lessen that intensity at all by affirming that John himself was the
Elijah whom the Jews believed would precede the
Messiah. Jesus said, "And if you are willing to accept it, he is the Elijah who was to come" (11:14).
Jesus knew that many people were not willing to
view John as a prophet because they did not want
to accept his authority or his ideas. But some did
have ears to hear this message.

Many did not have ears to hear, however, so Jesus then gave a parable (see also Luke 7:31-35)
saying that the present generation of people were
like children, some wanting to play the game of
funeral, and others wanting to play the game of
wedding. The two pretend games were interesting
contrasts because in the wedding game the children danced joyously and played instruments,
while in the funeral game the children mourned,
cried and sang a dirge. When John the ascetic
prophet came, the people preferred dancing and
being joyous. But when Jesus came preaching lib-

erty from legalism, the people wanted to mourn and fast. In other words, the fickle audience wanted neither John nor Jesus, and ultimately rejected the kingdom of God that both John and Jesus came to announce (see Matthew 3:2; 4:17).

Unrepentant Cities (Matthew 11:20-24)

Jesus then began to denounce some of the cities that were rejecting His ministry, even after observing His miracles. Korazin, Bethsaida and Capernaum were particularly cited as culpable, and even more culpable than Tyre, Sidon and Sodom. Their sin did not seem to have been outright rejection but merely indifference to the ministry of Jesus. Tyre and Sidon, Jesus said, would have repented in sackcloth and ashes had they witnessed the miracles that Jesus performed in Korazin and Bethsaida. Sodom, Jesus affirmed, would still exist if it had witnessed the miracles that Jesus performed in Capernaum. Against all three cities Jesus pronounced a message of doom and judgment. No doubt some people in these cities embraced the kingdom. Peter, for example, was a native of Capernaum. But the judgment upon these people would be severe because they were given the privilege of seeing what so many others can only dream about, namely, the supernatural deeds that attest the presence of God.

Jesus and the Lowly (Matthew 11:25-30)

Why did the people of these cities not respond to the ministry of Jesus? The ensuing prayer from

Jesus to His Father (11:25-26) suggests that God chose to hide spiritual realities from those who considered themselves to be wise and learned, while revealing them to those who were more humble like little children. This suggests that the qualification for discerning divine wisdom is not intellect and high standing, but moral sensitivity. We should note, however, that Jesus was not here promoting a necessary relationship between ignorance and religious faith. The most intelligent of people may very well have a strong moral and spiritual sensitivity, while the less intelligent people may also have hard hearts and an unwarranted sense of pride.

Alfred Plummer calls verse 27 the premier Christological passage in the synoptic gospels.[2] The Father-Son terminology is more typically Johannine, but Plummer assures us that these words recorded by Matthew are very authentic. The essence of verse 27 emphasizes strongly the sovereignty of both the Father and the Son, who will be known only at their own good pleasure. The necessity for supernatural revelation of the identity of both Father and Son may conflict with our desire to be in control and have the ability to achieve our spiritual goals. However, the Father has given authority to the Son to reveal or withhold knowledge of the Father.

Then Jesus offered a most gracious invitation to those who were following Him. Jesus invited them as weary and burdened people to come to Him. He would give them rest by helping to carry their burden. Often these verses are taken to imply that the load of sin would be left on Jesus, but that does not fit the context. Rather, Jesus was telling His disciples to cast off the harsh Pharisaic expectations (similar to Matthew 23:4) and live by a different principle—one that is comparatively easy and light. Often in Jewish writing the ox yoke was used as a metaphor for the obligation of the law. Possibly the easy yoke that Jesus refers to in verse 30 was the Jubilee lifestyle that He called His disciples to follow.

The description Jesus gave of Himself as being gentle and humble in heart, and the invitation for His followers to learn from Him, indicate that these qualities are at the heart and soul of kingdom living. The gentle and humble, rather than the forceful and proud, are better suited for the lifestyle of the kingdom.

Criticism from the Pharisees: Sabbath Observance (Matthew 12:1-21)

In chapter 12 we see four controversies in which the Pharisees were critical of Jesus. In each conflicting story it is helpful to ask crucial questions: "What scruple is being violated and why?" "What expectation is not being met?" "By what principle is Jesus acting?" And, "How did Jesus correct the misunderstanding?" A summary question that helps apply the teachings to our lives is, "What does this passage teach us about how we should relate to the scruples of others?" We saw in the previous narrative section (Matthew 8 and 9)

that in Jesus the kingdom was confronting the unclean. In this section we see Jesus being confronted by the so-called clean. His successful
ministry to the unclean and His successful rejoin-
ders to the so-called clean are evidence that in a
unique way, the Spirit of God ministered through
the Son of God to all sorts of people.

Chapter 12 relates the first strong volley of hostile ammunition from the Pharisees against Jesus.
Their criticism touches four topics: Sabbath observance (12:1-8), Sabbath healing (vv. 9-21),
working for Satan (12:22-37) and the use of signs
(12:38-45).

The first criticism was offered by the Pharisees
against the disciples who were walking through
the grainfields picking the heads of grain to eat.
The Pharisees accused them of doing what was
unlawful to do on a Sabbath. Foraging for food in
a neighbor's field actually was allowed, according
to Deuteronomy 23:25. The objection of the
Pharisees was that this was being done on a Sabbath. They considered plucking the heads of grain
and rubbing them to be a form of reaping, threshing, and winnowing and, therefore, to be unnecessary work on a Sabbath. In reply, Jesus gave two
illustrations to indicate that the ceremonial law
must give way to the higher claims of charity and
compassion. David and his men in a time of extreme hunger actually took the consecrated shew-
bread from the house of God. Likewise, temple
priests were allowed by the law to "break the Sabbath" and remain guiltless. Jesus then offended

His listeners by stating that in their immediate presence was something far greater than even the temple. He may have been referring to Himself, or perhaps to the presence of the kingdom in Himself and His disciples. Jesus then cited the familiar verse from Hosea 6:6 (already quoted in Matthew 9:13) in which God indicates that He prefers mercy to sacrifice. Then Jesus made the seemingly audacious claim that as the Son of Man, He was also Lord of the Sabbath. No doubt, this did little to endear Him to the Pharisees.

From the field Jesus and His followers went into a local synagogue where they met a man with a withered hand. The Pharisees took the opportunity to ask Jesus whether it was lawful to heal on the Sabbath. According to Matthew, their intent was to catch Him doing something wrong. The patriarch Jerome said that in a form of the gospel used by the Nazarenes and Ebionites, the man with the withered hand took the initiative by saying to Jesus, "I was a mason earning my bread with my hands. I pray thee, Jesu, restore my health that I may not in shame beg for food."[3] In Mark's account of this incident (Mark 3:1-6), Jesus asked the Pharisees whether it was lawful on the Sabbath to do good or evil, or to save life or kill it. Because they remained silent, Jesus looked at them in anger and was deeply grieved about their hard hearts. The incident is a striking example of the Pharisees' preferring formalism to principle. Jesus might have argued that stretching out the hand was not a breach of the Sabbath. Rather, He used the broad principle that to heal is to do good and, therefore, is a proper observance of the Sabbath. If, through self-interest, a person was allowed to retrieve a sheep that had fallen into a pit on the Sabbath, then certainly restoring a human to health would be a noble and lawful deed. His talk then turned to action as He commanded the man to stretch out his hand. The man's obedience resulted in his healing. The healing, however, resulted in the Pharisees leaving the synagogue and beginning to plot how they might destroy Jesus.

Knowing His immediate danger, Jesus left that vicinity. Even as He did so, He continued to heal people along the way. Wanting to minimize the possibility of trouble, Jesus warned those who were healed not to publicize their healings or make Him known. Matthew indicates that Jesus, by maintaining the secrecy of His identity, was fulfilling the words of one of the Servant Songs from Isaiah (Isaiah 42:1-4). Here we see Matthew identifying the Messiah as a servant. It was the Jews' failure to make this identification that ultimately led to their complete misunderstanding of the identity of Jesus. In their minds, a suffering servant could not also be the Messiah. By using this Servant Song, Matthew was affirming that Jesus would conquer without violence.

Perhaps another focus of this text is the emphasis on the Gentiles with whom Jesus would have an effective ministry. In contrast to the Jewish leaders who were hardening their hearts against the ministry of Jesus, verses 18 and 21 indicate that the Gentiles would be responsive.

Accused of Working with Beelzebub (Matthew 12:22-37)

The Pharisees criticized Jesus a third time after Jesus healed a demon-possessed man who was blind and dumb. When the healed man began to speak and see, the amazed crowds began to wonder whether Jesus was the "Son of David," which was a messianic title. To discredit this notion, the Pharisees said that Jesus was casting out the demons by using the power of Beelzebub, the archdemon. A quote from Alfred Plummer indicates the importance of what was occurring here.

> But what is important for us is that this charge of Christ's being in league with Satan proves that there was something extraordinary to explain. If there had not been mighty works too remarkable to ignore and too notorious to deny, His enemies would never have taken refuge in so extravagant an hypothesis. This charge must be set side by side with the Jewish tradition that Jesus had brought charms out of Egypt, or had learnt magic from Egyptian sorcerers. In both cases we have evidence, unintentionally given, in support of the miracles wrought by Christ.[4]

Jesus' compelling logic in verses 25-29 put to silence the foolish suggestion of the Pharisees. But Jesus did not stop there. Verses 30-32 indicate the impossibility of being in a position of neutrality regarding the ministry of Jesus. By not being for Him, the Pharisees were against Him and, therefore, they were the ones who were in alliance with Satan. This is a test that each person must apply to himself or herself. If we cannot say that we are on Christ's side, then indeed, we are against Him.

We now come to one of the most difficult sayings in the Bible, namely, the statement in verse 31 that there is a sin so heinous that it is unforgivable. Jesus describes it as "blasphemy against the Spirit." Jesus explains that while speaking against the Son of Man is forgivable, those who speak against the Holy Spirit will not be forgiven. These verses relate directly to the charge of the Pharisees that Jesus was doing His work by the power of Satan. Attributing the Spirit's work to Satan was the unpardonable sin. Misunderstanding philanthropic works such as those done by Jesus is pardonable, though deplorable. We may believe that one spontaneous careless act of the tongue is not what Jesus would consider to be an unforgivable sin—that would be more the spirit of legalism than the Spirit of Christ. The unforgivable sin was a sin that came from a twisted character that called "good" evil and "evil" good.

The succeeding verses, which refer to good and bad trees and good and bad fruit, recall verses from the Sermon on the Mount (Matthew 7:17-19). The Pharisees did not doubt that the effect of the ministry of Jesus was good, but they attacked the source, saying that a good effect was coming from an evil source. Jesus made it quite clear here that both the cause and effect are either good or evil. Evil people could produce nothing but evil fruit, particularly the fruit of their words. That is why in verse 34 Jesus called the Pharisees a "brood of vipers." The poison that came from these people was the careless word that put them in danger of judgment. Words reveal the intent of the heart and the character of a person, and that is why they form a legitimate basis for God's judgment.

Sign Seeking (Matthew 12:38-45)

Perhaps to deflect the heat of the moment, or to push Jesus into greater frustration with them, some scribes and Pharisees asked that Jesus perform a sign, or an attesting miracle to give evidence of His identity. Jesus called these people an evil and adulterous generation and said that no sign would be given to them, presumably because the Pharisees had already rejected His beneficent miracles. Apparently, they were looking for some kind of power sign, such as altering nature, or doing some special creative act. Jesus, instead, said they would only receive the sign of Jonah the prophet.

In referring to Jonah, Jesus brought several ideas to mind. First, Jonah preached and his audience responded positively. Also, Jonah was, in a sense, "buried" for three days and then "resurrected." Jesus also preached, but His audience hardened their hearts. Also, Jesus predicted that

He, like Jonah, would spend three days in death and subsequently be resurrected. That would be the coveted sign the Pharisees would need. Yet when it happened, they would not respond positively to it. We must note that verses 41 and 42, if they were not uttered by the Son of God, would be the extreme height of arrogance. Only Jesus could utter these words and be credible doing it. Jesus was certainly greater than Jonah, greater than any of the Old Testament characters.

Verses 43-45 return to the untenable idea that one can be neutral with regard to Jesus and the kingdom of God. Presumably, the demon-possessed man in verse 22 who had been restored from his blindness and dumbness was still present. So the imagery Jesus used was appropriate. This man, like any cured from demonic possession, would need something to replace the demons. The Pharisees had nothing to offer. We must assume that Jesus ministered the rest of the gospel to this man.

Some see a possible second meaning in this reference to the unclean spirits seeking to find a place of rest and eventually reoccupying their former dwelling with seven other spirits. Israel had become free from idolatry but had more recently become trapped by the legalism of Pharisaism, another form of spiritual tyranny. Others see that perhaps Jesus was referring to those who began as followers of John the Baptist, but who were in danger of rejecting the messiahship of Jesus. They would be easy prey for demonic or Pharisaic influence.

Family Caution (Matthew 12:46-50)

The last episode in this narrative is equally surprising to all that has preceded it. The mother and brothers of Jesus had come to the scene and were seeking to talk with Jesus. He seems callused when He asks, "Who is my mother, and who are my brothers?" This should not be taken as denying His mother and brothers as members of His family, or denying His affection for them. Rather, Jesus strongly affirms that the kingdom is of the utmost priority for Him so that those who do the will of the heavenly Father are to be considered the family of Jesus. The idea here is similar to the hyperbole found in Luke 12:49-53, where Jesus mentioned that His coming would split apart families. The ideas in Luke 14:26 are similar. Jesus maintained that whoever tried to come and follow Him without hating his father, mother, wife, children, brothers, sisters or even his own life could not be a disciple of Jesus. Clearly, this is hyperbole because we know that Jesus was very tenderly attached to His own family. Nevertheless, the urgency of the kingdom made all earthly intimacies pale in comparison to the passion with which Jesus went about His ministry. As it was with Jesus, so it would need to be with His disciples.

Endnotes

1. Plummer, p. 160.

2. Ibid., p. 166.
3. Jerome [quoted by Plummer, page 174, foot-
   note].
4. Plummer, p. 176.

CHAPTER 6

Kingdom Parables

Matthew 13:1-52

Jesus was a one-message Man. His main sermon theme was the kingdom of God. He began with it (Matthew 4:17, Mark 1:14), and He ended with it (Acts 1:3). The kingdom of God is the dominant theme of the New Testament Gospels. Mark used the phrase "kingdom of God" 14 times; Luke used it 32 times; and Matthew mentioned "kingdom of God" 4 times and the synonymous "kingdom of heaven" 33 times.

The concept of the kingdom of God does not reduce to one simple statement; indeed, Jesus spent His three years of public ministry defining the kingdom of God. He did this both through direct teaching and through examples of life. Most of the parables He told are parables of the kingdom.

Seven parables of Jesus are found in Matthew 13. These parables all have the same theme: the kingdom of God. Parables communicate effectively by using word pictures to make abstract truth concrete. They start with what people know and move them toward what they do not yet know. They compel interest because of their local and visual connection. Parables allow people to discover truth for themselves, and conceal truth from those who are too lazy to think or too blinded by prejudice.

Studies on the interpretation of parables suggest that parables usually teach only one point. When a parable is exceptionally apt, we tend to treat it as an allegory, trying to find one-to-one correspondences between the image and the reality being discussed. This practice may lead to fanciful ideas never intended by Jesus. Occasionally He interpreted a parable like an analogy. The parable of the four kinds of soil in Matthew 13:3-9 and its explanation in verses 18-23 illustrate this. When that is not done, however, it is far better to be cautious with the imagery than to interpret the parable as an allegory.

By using a thematic rather than a chronological structure, Matthew brings together seven parables, which are scattered in the other synoptic Gospels. For purposes of reference, we will list the seven parables here and indicate where the parallel passages are found.

Parable	Matthew	Mark	Luke
1. The Sower and Soils	13:1-23	4:3-9	8:4-18
2. The Tares and Wheat	3:24-31	4:26	-
3. The Mustard Seed	13:31-32	4:30-32	13:18-19
4. The Leaven	13:33	-	13:20-21
5. The Hidden Treasure	13:44	-	-
6. The Costly Pearl	13:45-46	-	-
7. The Dragnet	13:47-50	-	-

The Sower and Soils (Matthew 13:1-23)

The message Jesus communicated through this parable was so important that all three synoptic Gospel writers record it. Although the lesson is quite simple, this parable received special treatment by being carefully interpreted by Jesus in verses 18-23.

The message was simply that the human soul may be compared to various types of soil in which the seed, or the Word of God, is scattered. Perhaps as Jesus gave this parable He was able to point toward a field where a farmer was walking along the field scattering seed.

The first kind of soil was the hardened paths in the fields on which the farmer and others would walk. Some of the seed would fall on this hardened path. Jesus mentioned that the birds of the air would come and eat this seed. When He gave the interpretation later in the chapter, He mentioned that the birds are like the evil one who comes and snatches away what was sown in a person's heart.

The second kind of soil was rocky. The depth of soil was not great enough to sustain adequate root growth. Therefore, the energy of the soil, the sun and the water went into the plant above the surface, where immediate growth was seen but not sustained. The sun came up and the plant withered because the root network did not provide adequate nourishment. Jesus said that this soil is like the person who receives the Word of

God immediately with great joy, but when persecution and trouble come the person withers in his faith.

The third kind of soil is infested with thorns. The seed germinates, sprouts and grows up, but along with its growth come many thorns that eventually choke out the good plant. Jesus said that the soil with thorns is like a person whose life is preoccupied with cares and worries and charmed by the wealth of the world, which chokes out the spiritual seed.

The fourth, and final, kind of soil about which Jesus spoke was the good soil. It was receptive to the seed and produced a crop many times greater than what was sown. Jesus said this soil is like a person who hears the Word of God and understands it and bears fruit in his life.

Let's look more closely at these four soils. In the more primitive days before modern farm machinery, cultivating, sowing and reaping had to be done by hand. Sometimes animals assisted, but sowing the seed was left to the individual farmer who walked the paths of his field scattering the seed. The paths that were trod could be as hard as pavement—like a person with a closed mind whose prejudice is so great that his spirit is unteachable, perhaps due to pride or fear of new truth. To be prejudiced means to have issues prejudged so that there's no room for negotiation or even learning new insights. Many individuals fit this category. The Word of God, despite its vigor and potential for bearing great fruit, will never take root in the life of a person like this. They have already determined what they want to believe and, perhaps, have even dismissed the Word of God as being irrelevant. The person's loss is his soul, which gets snatched up by the evil one.

The rocky soil is particularly interesting. Often we think of it as soil containing a lot of rocks, but Jesus was referring to soil only a few inches deep covering a layer of limestone. This soil may be compared to a person with a flighty mind who refuses to think deeply and thoroughly. These are people who enjoy a fad or a craze, people for whom form is more important than substance, people for whom emotional appeal is far preferable to a reasoned appeal. This type of soil is deceptive because on the surface it appears as good as any other soil. It's all the more deceptive because evidence of life appears immediately from the seed. However, the lack of a root system soon forces the untimely death of the plant before fruit has been produced. Some people who receive the Word of God eagerly and embrace it wholeheartedly end up abandoning their new faith because they have not considered the full implications of its life-transforming power. Some people use Christianity simply as a panacea for their immediate problem, and when their problem is solved, they quickly revert to their former lifestyle and belief system. On another occasion, Jesus said that unless a seed falls into the ground and dies, it cannot bear fruit. People of shallow soil are not willing for the seed to die and, therefore, are not really ever able to bear fruit.

The thorny soil is also deceptive because it looks clean but is crowded with competing seeds. Like a busy, cluttered life, the thorny soil is filled with many activities that claim a person's attention and affection. The current pursuit of self-actualizing and self-fulfilling activities is an example of thorns in a person's life. New Age religion is another example. At best, the kingdom of God is an add-on to such a person's life. Jesus mentioned that the thorns are like the worries of this life and the deceitfulness of wealth. Again we have a situation where the implications of the fullness of the kingdom of God and its expectations for its followers are not readily comprehended.

Finally, the fertile soil is completely unlike the other three. It is unlike the hardened path because it is soft. It is unlike the rocky soil because it is deep. It is unlike the thorny soil because it is clean. This type of person is prepared to hear, understand and obey the teaching of the kingdom.

Jesus finished the parable by saying, "He who has ears, let him hear" (13:43). The intention of this comment, obviously, is that there is much below the surface of this story that needs to be understood and appropriated in a person's life.

Although the disciples were fascinated by the parable, they were also a bit skeptical about the practicality of speaking to the people in such an enigmatic way. Jesus did little to erase their question by giving them a response that was similarly enigmatic. He mentioned that the kingdom of

God has certain secrets or mysteries that are available to some people, but unavailable to others. In fact, He added that those who have some knowledge of the kingdom would be given an abundance, but those who have little knowledge will be deprived even of what they have. Then Jesus cited verses from Isaiah 6 in which the prophet mentioned that the people of God in that day would have many opportunities to hear and to see, but because their hearts were hardened, they were closing themselves off to the truth. In God's sovereign plan, those whose hearts have been callused have chosen to reject the ways of God, and therefore, God does not let them in on the secrets of the kingdom. He purposely does not want those with hardened hearts to hear and understand the message.

It is important to understand here that the hardened heart precedes the activity of God in withholding the kingdom secrets from these people. The disciples, unlike the people in Isaiah's day and the other people who also heard the parable, were able to see and hear and perceive the truth because their hearts were soft and they were teachable. Jesus mentioned that many great people in the past—prophets and other righteous individuals—eagerly longed to see and hear what the disciples were now experiencing. In other words, Jesus was saying to the disciples that this message was the one that the prophets of old knew would come through God's chosen Messiah.

Through this parable Jesus communicated various messages. He communicated a message of encouragement. Seeds from the Word of God will be sown, find suitable soil in which to grow and produce a wonderful crop called the kingdom of God. Jesus also offered a message of realism in that He clearly stated that not everyone will be responsive to the Word of God. Nevertheless, the disciples should be persistent because the seed needs to be sown, regardless of the unresponsiveness of some people. Jesus also brought a message about patience. It takes a long time for the seed to bear fruit, but there is life in the seed, and eventually that seed would sprout in the right soil and bear the fruit of the kingdom of God. Therefore, the message is also one of great hope to the disciples.

The Tares and Wheat (Matthew 13:24-30)

Staying with agrarian imagery, Jesus told a second parable about a man who sowed good seed in his field. The soil was good soil, but an enemy came during the night and sowed darnel seeds, which in the early stages would produce a weed very similar in appearance to wheat. The grain of the darnel is very bitter and slightly poisonous. This nasty trick was sometimes done by an enemy. After the darnel and the wheat seeds matured, it would be evident that a bad deed had been done and that an enemy had corrupted the field.

The servants in the story asked the owner whether they should try to pull up the darnel plants. The owner responded that they should not disturb the field because the wheat would likely be pulled up along with the darnel. The recommendation was to let both grow and be harvested. During the time of harvesting, the darnel would be removed from the wheat and tied in bundles to be burned, while the wheat would be harvested and stored in the barn.

The lesson is that the kingdom of God grows side by side with the kingdom of evil, but that separation and retribution will come at the appropriate time of harvesting. This was an important message for the disciples because, given their religious heritage and understanding, it was assumed that if the Messiah were in their presence, then they must be living in the messianic age, characterized by the triumph of righteousness over evil. Since Jesus knew that the kingdom would not appear this way, He taught the disciples to be patient, hopeful and persistent in their service for God in the kingdom.

The Mustard Seed (Matthew 13:31-32)

Matthew also compared the kingdom of God to a mustard seed, which, although very small, produces a huge tree that hosts the birds of the air. While the mustard seed was proverbial for its smallness, it could grow into a large tree about 12 feet high with large branches. In Matthew 17:20 Jesus compared faith to a mustard seed: |A disciple's faith might start as small as a mustard seed, but result in something of great magnitude. The birds that perch in its branches may allude to the

Gentiles, as it often does elsewhere in Scripture. Thus, Jesus may have meant that the kingdom of God will welcome many from the Gentile world.

The lesson is clear: the kingdom of God starts out very small, but advances persistently.

The Yeast (Matthew 13:33)

In a similar parable Jesus mentioned that the kingdom is like yeast that a woman mixed into a large amount of flour, working it through the dough. The image was easily understood in those days. Usually a woman would withhold a small piece of dough from being baked and allow it to ferment. It would then become leaven, or yeast, and be mixed in with the next batch of baking to be done. The leaven would cause the entire clump of dough to rise into a larger loaf. Without leaven, the bread would be flat, hard and unsavory.

Often in the New Testament leaven refers to an evil influence. Contrary to what some have thought, the unleavened bread associated with the Passover lacked leaven only because the Hebrews did not have time to wait for it to rise during their hasty departure from Egypt (Exodus 12:39). It was not because of any association with evil or sin. Such is the case here in Matthew 13:33. Here leaven stands for a latent, transforming power that will have an effect far greater than its own size.

Similar to the previous parable, the lesson of this parable is that the kingdom of God will spread throughout society and exert a transform- ing influence on it. Without the kingdom the culture is flat, insipid and virtually useless. The disciples should not despair about the size of the kingdom or the number of its disciples because its influence will be far greater than initial appearances would suggest.

At this point, Matthew interrupts the parables to explain that Jesus was speaking to the crowd using parables to fulfill a prophecy in Psalm 78:2 that said, "I will open my mouth in parables, I will utter things hidden since the creation of the world." As we have already seen, reference to the fulfillment of Old Testament prophecies is common in the Gospel of Matthew.

An Interpretation (Matthew 13:36-43)

Although Jesus had just finished telling the fourth parable, the disciples were still pondering the second parable. When the crowds left and the disciples and Jesus went into a house, they asked Him to explain the parable of the wheat and tares. He followed with another point-by-point allegorical interpretation of a parable. Jesus specifically said that the one who sows the good seed is the Son of Man; the field is the world; the good seed stands for the sons of the kingdom, while the weeds are the sons of the evil one. The enemy who sows the seeds of the weeds is the devil. The harvest, He said, is the end of the age and the harvesters are the angels.

The point of the parable is that when the weeds are pulled up, they will be burned in the fire, whereas the good seed will be separated from the

weeds. The imagery Jesus used about the end of
the age is quite alarming. Matthew 13:41 indicates
that the Son of Man will send out the angels who
will weed out of the kingdom everything that
causes sin and all who do evil. They will be
thrown into a fiery furnace where there will be
"weeping and gnashing of teeth." The righteous,
however, will enjoy a much more favorable future
in the kingdom of their Father. Jesus then repeats,
"He who has ears, let him hear." Alfred Plummer
notes that this phrase is sometimes misunderstood
as referring to "a favoured minority, gifted with
special intelligence as to spiritual truth, or as referring to those who are *willing* to hear. *All* have ears;
and therefore all are responsible for refusing to listen. A man cannot plead that he was *unable* to
hear. The word was brought to him and he rejected it."[1]

The Hidden Treasure (Matthew 13:44)

To tell the last three parables Jesus left the boat
and entered a house. Only the disciples were with
Him. He continued by telling them about a hidden treasure. In this short parable a very valuable
possession was hidden in a field. A man found the
treasure and hid it again before others could discover it. Then, out of great joy and longing for
that valuable possession, he sold everything in order to buy the field so that the treasure would
rightfully be his.

In the first-century it was not unusual for people to hide their treasure. For example, the parable

of the talents tells about a lazy servant who went out and buried the one talent he had been given (25:25). This was not just a first-century practice, however. I personally know a family of Vietnamese refugees who did something similar. The wife, who came from a wealthy family, told us that before coming to the United States, her family had buried many gold bars in a hillside in South Vietnam.

The lesson of this parable is that the kingdom of God is the most valuable possession a person can have. It outweighs all other blessings and is, therefore, worthy of total sacrifice. The fact that the man was joyfully willing to sell everything he possessed to buy the field indicates the high value he placed upon the treasure. In the parable, the treasure, of course, is the kingdom.

The Costly Pearl (Matthew 13:45-46)

In verse 45 Jesus compared the kingdom of heaven to a merchant who was looking for fine pearls. At last he found one of great value and went away and sold everything he owned to be able to purchase the one excellent pearl. People in ancient times greatly admired pearls for both their economic and aesthetic properties. When a person was handling an exceptionally valuable pearl, he would have a sense of tremendous joy simply by pondering that pearl, holding it and showing it off to other people. Great pearls were found mostly on the shores of the Red Sea and in faraway Britain. So, truly valuable pearls were imported.

The lesson of this parable is similar to the previous one. Once the valuable treasure was discovered, the person was willing to sacrifice every thing to obtain it. In this case, however, he searched for the pearl carefully, whereas in the previous parable he found the hidden treasure in the field unexpectedly. Without trying to allegorize these parables, we suggest that some people find the kingdom of God without a personal and conscious search, whereas others exercise great care in exploring various belief systems and only after much effort come upon the pearl of the kingdom.

The Dragnet (Matthew 13:47-50)

The last parable in this series is drawn from the imagery of fishing. In early times fishermen engaged in two kinds of fishing. The first was the exclusive type of fishing in which the fisherman sought to catch a specific kind of fish. The other kind of fishing was the inclusive kind in which the fisherman used a huge net to gather all kinds of sea life, including much that would be useless. This net was called a "dragnet" because it was dragged along the bottom of the sea. Eventually, the fishermen hauled it to shore where they separated the fish. In the parable Jesus told, the net caught "all kinds of fish." The fishermen sat down and separated the good fish from the bad. Jesus mentioned that the parable illustrated the end time when the angels will come and separate the wicked from the righteous.

The lesson is similar to the parable of the tares and wheat, where both the good and bad plants were harvested and then separated. The kingdom of God grows and lives in the midst of an ungodly world. The consummation of history will result in the final separation and discarding of that which no longer has value to the kingdom.

The reference to a fiery furnace and weeping and gnashing of teeth in the second and seventh parables is an offensive image to many. The thought that a loving God would send humans to a place of perpetual torment is repugnant. Nevertheless, the Scriptures are as clear on this teaching as they are on any other teaching. Our problem is that we begin our consideration of the issue from a man-centered basis. In our subjectivity and self-centeredness, we ignore the unholiness of an unredeemed soul. The human soul has been created to worship God and enjoy God's presence, and yet it refuses to worship God. Being unable to fulfill its only purpose for eternity, that soul is then useless and profitless to the life of the kingdom of God. The only alternative is to be excluded from the kingdom and discarded.

One might say that is all quite logical. But why such a severe consequence? Is God vengeful and seeking to punish the rebellious soul? The answer is, "yes and no." God's wrath is revealed from heaven against all godlessness and wickedness (Romans 1:18); however, the wrath is not revealed against individuals, but against the properties of unrighteousness and ungodliness, which are incarnate in these individuals. Wherever sin is found, God deals with it in order to be just. Nevertheless, God is not vengeful in His desire to punish sin at the price of great pain for humans. The consequence of being separated from God at any time is total torment. We know from Scripture that God graciously provides the rain and the sun both for the just and the unjust (Matthew 5:45). When God removes the blessings of His presence and His provisions, that by itself is hell. Total deprivation of the blessing of the presence and provisions of God will result in sheer torment. It is inevitable. It cannot be any other way.

The Use of Parables

We have already seen in 13:10-17 and 34-35 that Matthew has reported comments by Jesus to describe the importance and role of the use of parables in communicating truths about the kingdom of heaven. Two ideas are very important for us to add, now that we have looked at all seven parables. The first focuses on the phrase Jesus used in 13:11, which is literally translated "mysteries of the kingdom." Jesus mentioned that only those who are insiders, or believers, would be able to understand such mysteries. In the first-century a mystery was a truth that was baffling to those who were on the outside, but readily understood by those on the inside. A modern example of this is the communion service. Not knowing the meaning of the elements, an unchurched observer would be totally puzzled by this practice. Why would adults sit in a church, spending precious time to ingest a small morsel of bread and a sip of wine or juice? Certainly these elements would do little to satisfy a person's hunger. The insider, of course, knows the mystery attached to this sacrament.

A second comment about the use of parables revolves around the idea that a person who already possesses some knowledge of the kingdom will be given an abundance, whereas those who have none or little will be deprived. This is simply a fact of life that is incontrovertible. A person who has some knowledge has the opportunity to build upon that knowledge. Take, for example, the subject of literacy. A person who knows how to read has far greater potential to learn an abundance of truth than a person who is illiterate. Likewise with a craft, a skill, or a language. A person who possesses an elementary ability has the potential to develop far greater skill, whereas the uninitiated would not even know where to begin.

The Message of the Parables

We have already seen that the parables have some similarities. All of them tell about the kingdom of heaven, or the kingdom of God. Jesus used these parables to teach four lessons. Parable one, which is about the four kinds of soil, teaches that the kingdom of God grows in a welcoming environment, but will not flourish in other contexts. Parables two and seven, the tares and the wheat and the dragnet, teach that the kingdom of God exists in the midst of evil but that separation is coming. Parables three and four, the mustard seed and the leaven, teach that the kingdom of God starts out small but has significant results. Parables five and six, the hidden treasure and the costly pearl, teach that the kingdom of God is very valuable and worthy of total sacrifice.

Treasures New and Old (Matthew 13:51-52)

This narrative ends with Jesus asking the disciples whether they "understood all these things." Surprisingly, we find them answering, "Yes." Earlier they were still pondering parable number two after Jesus had given them number four. Perhaps showing some naïveté, the disciples asserted with great confidence that they understood all the parables. Whereas in 13:10 the disciples questioned the appropriateness of using parables to teach spiritual truths to the people, now in verse 51 the disciples agreed that the parables had been effective. They understood the messages Jesus intended to communicate. Jesus accepted the diciples' response at face value without questioning.

Jesus' reply in 13:52 gave the disciples a very important mission. In verse 52 the word "therefore" means "well, then." Perhaps an expanded paraphrase of it would be "because you have been able to understand by means of parables." Jesus was indicating to the disciples that they themselves would teach the gospel by means of parabolic instruction. They were to be to the gospel what the scribes were to the law; they would produce for the benefit of their hearers, not merely the age-old truths given in the same old way, but they were to use old and familiar ideas to communicate truth to a new generation. Like Jesus, they would take the familiar phenomena of nature and use them to communicate spiritual truths.

We should not pass over this idea without exploring the very valuable commodity the church has in those people who have been brought up as believers from their childhood. Seminary presidents and professors are noting today the difficult task which is theirs in having to train people as pastors who have not been brought up in the church. Often individuals become Christians during their college years, sense a call of God to ministry and then proceed to seminary. Because they do not have old treasures from the wealth of spiritual background provided by Sunday school and church during younger years, it is more difficult for them than for others to gain ministry skills. The most valuable communicator of spiritual truth may well be the one who has treasures that are old as well as new. Nevertheless, it is abundantly clear that the scribe, without the new message of the kingdom, would be ill equipped to communicate effectively the most needed message, namely, the truth about the kingdom of heaven.

Endnotes

1. Plummer, p. 196.

CHAPTER 7

Kingdom Mentality for Disciples

Matthew 13:53-17:27

In each case the division between narrative and discourse sections of Matthew's Gospel occurs at chapter breaks, except for the fourth narrative section, which breaks between Matthew 13:52 and 13:53. We can be confident that this is a transition from discourse to narrative because the end of discourse formula used in all other cases is used here, namely, "when Jesus had finished (these parables)."

The fourth narrative section describes the itinerant ministry of Jesus. At first look, it seems to be a random sampling of encounters, ministries, conflicts and episodes. The tapestry of Matthew's Gospel, however, would lead us to believe that an intentional design can be found. Careful examination of the 16 episodes in this section reveals four dominant themes: (1) Jesus teaches kingdom mentality to the disciples; (2) Jesus highlights the importance of faith; (3) Jesus predicts His passion;

and (4) the primacy of Peter is unfolded. We will observe these four themes as we travel through these chapters.

Geographical Movement (Matthew 13:53-58)

While we have already noted that Matthew's Gospel is not a chronological account of the ministry of Jesus, it is interesting to note the variety of places where Jesus ministered and the impressive number of miles He and His disciples traveled. In these four chapters we find Him and His disciples in Nazareth, Gennesaret, the area of Tyre and Sidon, Capernaum, Caesarea Philippi, Mount Hermon and back in Galilee. These journeys took more than six months and included a significant amount of time in Gentile country.

No doubt on several occasions Jesus tried to minister to the people of His hometown, Nazareth. Luke 4 tells of one such incidence early in Jesus' ministry. On that occasion, after reading Scripture in the synagogue and applying a prophecy to Himself, Jesus was run out of town. Perhaps the account in Matthew 13:53-58 is the same occasion. The unbelief of the former neighbors of Jesus stifled His prophetic and miraculous ministry and caused Him to vacate the area. The people of Nazareth were truly impressed by the wisdom of Jesus, and they seemed to have heard of His miraculous deeds. Nevertheless, for them it was a stumbling block that Jesus was one of them. They knew His mother and His brothers and sisters, and in no way were they able to countenance the idea that One from among their own group would be chosen by God for such special ministry. With grief, and perhaps some indignation, Jesus quoted the proverb about a prophet being without honor only in his own home town and household.

The End of an Era (Matthew 14:1-12)

At the beginning of chapter 14, Matthew reports what had happened to John the Baptist. Herod the tetrarch had heard news about Jesus and assumed that John the Baptist must have risen from the dead. Two reasons may have fueled Herod's fears. First, the Jews believed that Elijah would return someday. Since it was commonly thought that John the Baptist may have been Elijah resurrected, Herod may have assumed that John the Baptist had supernatural endowments afforded to him. Because Herod had beheaded John, no doubt his guilt and fears were fueled by the stories of miraculous deeds being done throughout the countryside. Second, tradition says that Jesus and John the Baptist may have been very similar in appearance. So Herod, hearing about Jesus, feared John the Baptist was alive again.

Matthew's report of the events that led to the beheading of John the Baptist is consistent with the personality of John as we have come to know him. John's righteous indignation would not allow him to keep quiet about Herod stealing the wife of his brother Philip. Because he could not silence John about the adulterous relationship with Herodias, Herod put John in prison. Knowing that the people regarded John to be a prophet, Herod was reluctant to put John to death. Herodias had a different intention, however, and when the occasion of Herod's birthday came, she used the seductive dancing of her daughter to beguile Herod into promising to behead John the Baptist. Although Herod was upset that he had promised to put John to death, he caved in to social pressure rather than obeying the moral law and sparing the innocent life of John.

After learning about their master's fate, the disciples of John courageously came to retrieve the body to bury it. Then they reported the tragedy to Jesus. The impact on Jesus of John's execution was enormous. On several occasions in the next few sections we find Jesus seeking solitude, no doubt to grieve the loss of the man who was His prophetic forerunner and to ponder His own fate.

John and Elijah had been compared frequently. In fact, Jesus mentioned to the disciples that John the Baptist was, indeed, the "second coming" of Elijah. Also, the relationship between Ahab, Jezebel and Elijah is noticeably similar to that between Herod, Herodias and John. Elijah's fate was far better, but certainly not because of any clemency on the part of Ahab and Jezebel.

Feeding 5,000

(Matthew 14:13-21)

All four Gospels report this episode in which Jesus ministered compassionately to the hungry multitude who were following Him, listening to His teaching and seeking His healing. Although Jesus needed solitude, He did not refuse the clamoring crowd from receiving His ministry. The disciples, perhaps, were being sensitive to the need of Jesus by requesting that He send the multitudes away so that they might buy food in the village. Instead of doing that, Jesus commissioned the disciples to provide for the people in a way that they could not even imagine. Plummer notes that through the apostles the human race is fed, starting with this feeding of the 5,000. That the miracle was not psychological gimmickry is attested by the 12 remaining baskets full of food, more than the original amount. Some have considered the story to be a baseless legend or a religious allegory. But Plummer mentions, "It is impossible, on critical principles, to eliminate this miracle from the Gospel story, or to explain it away."[1]

While compassion certainly motivated Jesus, we may be certain that showing the disciples His awesome power and ability to provide was also paramount in His intentions. Presumably Jesus might have had the people come to Him to receive the food directly from His hands. Instead, He had the people sit on the grass. He then took the five loaves and two fish, blessed them and distributed them to the disciples, who redistributed them to the multitudes. Clearly, the disciples were meant to be part of the miraculous ministry.

Walking on Water (Matthew 14:22-33)

Still seeking solitude, Jesus sent the multitudes away and compelled the disciples to take a boat to the other side of the sea. Alone now, He ascended the mountains to pray. John's Gospel indicates that Jesus took such quick and decisive action because He understood that the crowd was ready to make Him king (John 6:15). Plummer notes that there was a tradition that the Messiah would feed the people with bread from heaven, as Moses had done in the wilderness. Indeed, Jesus had fed the people in the wilderness with bread that came in a more miraculous way.[2] Their deduction was logical and their enthusiasm was natural. At this point Jesus was at the height of His popularity. From this point foward, however, it began to diminish rapidly.

As the disciples were rowing the boat across the sea, a storm began to overtake them in the middle of the night. The Sea of Galilee is known for both the suddenness and the severity of storms. Some have suggested that the wind had pushed the boat near the shoreline and the disciples, not realizing they were close to the shore, saw Jesus walking in the shallow water and assumed He was walking on the water. This attempt to avoid the miraculous element of the story, however, fails when we consider several facts: (1) the disciples were "a considerable distance from land," perhaps three to four miles; and (2) Peter began to sink as he tried to walk on the water.

As we try to understand this episode, we may consider the possibility that Jesus was attempting again to teach the disciples a lesson about faith. His delay was similar to His delay in going to Lazarus who had died. Jesus wanted the full impact of the lesson to occur in each case—at the moment of greatest despair and helplessness the disciples will find in Jesus all the necessary resources to overcome a seemingly insurmountable problem. In this episode we also find Matthew's emphasis on Peter. His impetuous character in this story is consistent with his character during the week of passion. The emphasis on Peter is coupled with an emphasis on faith. While these lessons were difficult to learn, we are gratified by reading in John 21:1-14 that Peter, indeed, was a teachable disciple.

Many sermons about the walking-on-the-water incident point to Peter's fearfulness and lack of faith as he began to sink. Indeed, Jesus did reprimand him, calling him a man of little faith; however, Jesus was also probably quite proud of him—the other 11 remained in the boat. All of them benefited from the lesson because when Jesus got into the boat, the wind immediately stopped and those who were in the boat "worshiped Him, saying, 'Truly you are the Son of God'" (Matthew 14:33).

The Gennesaret Healings (Matthew 14:34-36)

The eventful crossing took them to Gennesaret on the east side of the Sea of Galilee. This area was inhabited by a mixture of ethnic groups, and we may assume that Jesus ministered in this area

on more than one occasion. Verse 35 says that the
men of that area recognized Jesus and invited
many to come who needed the healing touch of
Jesus. Matthew reports that even those who
touched the fringe of His cloak were restored to
health.

The Challenge by the Pharisees (Matthew 15:1-20)

Of all areas where we would not expect to find
Pharisees, Gennesaret was certainly such a place.
The Pharisees, however, were very eager at this
time to put an end to the ministry of Jesus. Perhaps because the popularity of Jesus in Galilee
was so strong, they thought they could more easily deal with Him in the Transjordan area. The
Pharisees started by accusing the disciples of Jesus
of not washing their hands ceremonially prior to
eating. Jesus did not respond to this charge directly. Instead, in verse 3 He put the spotlight on
the Pharisees by asking, "And why do you break
the command of God for the sake of your tradition?" Then to strengthen His comment, He said,
"For God saai . . . ," after which He quoted the
commandment about honoring father and mother.

We might think that this was an argument in
which Jesus would easily prevail. We should note,
however, that oral law often had a greater authority for the Jews than the written law. The reason
for this is that oral law preceded the written law.
Jesus said that the Pharisees employed the *Corban*
formula (Mark 7:11; Matthew 15:5 refers to this as

"a gift devoted to God") for one of several possible reasons. Perhaps just out of sheer greed, some of the Pharisees used this ritualistic saying to avoid having to give their parents any support. They could always appeal to the law to exempt themselves from being generous or even humane to their parents, covering it with a veneer of piety. The second possibility is that in a moment of heated anger a person might make an oath that would declare their property exempt from being used generously for their parents. Later they might try to recant from this oath, but the Pharisees would enforce it as binding and even more binding than the moral law of being generous.

In reality, this was not a clash between Jesus and the Pharisees but between two views of religion, or two views of the demands of God. The Pharisees were offended and shocked by the response of Jesus because the very heart of their religion was being attacked. Their shock became outrage when Jesus quoted Isaiah 29 to demonstrate their hypocrisy. The key phrase in the quote, however, was that God said the people were worshiping Him in vain because they taught the precepts of men as if they were doctrines. No wonder the disciples took Jesus aside and remonstrated with Him about offending the Pharisees (Matthew 15:12). The principle that Jesus taught was indeed radical, that people are defiled more by the words they use than the food they choose.

Jesus was not overly concerned about offending the Pharisees, calling them "blind guides" and perhaps comparing them to the tares mentioned in Matthew 13. Because they were not planted by the heavenly Father, they would be rooted up. Although they were offended by Jesus, the Pharisees were actually the ones who were causing others to stumble. Ultimately, the heavenly Father would uproot them so that they would no longer cause other people to stumble.

Peter took the initiative to ask Jesus to explain the parable about the difference between food that does not defile and words that do. The application Jesus gave was that food enters and exits the body harmlessly, even if it is eaten with unwashed hands. However, evil thoughts, murder, adultery, fornication, theft, bearing false witness and slandering—things that truly defile a person—proceed out of the mouth and the heart of an individual. The Pharisees seemed to care very little about such defilement and majored only on possible violations of their ceremonial law.

Ministry to a Canaanite Woman (Matthew 15:21-28)

In Matthew 15:21 we again see Jesus trying to escape the clamor of the public, this time by traveling quite a distance northwest to Tyre and Sidon, in an area close to the Mediterranean Sea, formerly called Phoenicia. The woman who approached Him is called a Canaanite whose ancestors were driven out of the Promised Land by Joshua. She addressed Jesus with an astonishing title, calling Him the "Son of David." No doubt this arrested His attention so that she could go on to explain her problem, namely, that her daughter was being tormented by a cruel demon. The text says that Jesus refused to answer her; apparently she made quite a nuisance out of herself to the point where the disciples were begging Jesus to send her away. Presumably, knowing the compassionate nature of Jesus, they were beseeching Him to go ahead and heal the girl so that the woman would be on her way.

Their concern was that they were being inconvenienced. Jesus' concern, however, was His special mission to Israel. That is why He responded with what seems to be a calloused answer. By referring to her as a dog it may seem that this was a grave insult. The term, however, does not indicate a filthy, foraging dog but a puppy owned by a family. Nevertheless, Jesus was declining her request. By saying that it was not right to take bread from the children to give it to the dog, Jesus was testing her attitude. Rather than being derailed into a discussion about ethnic pride, the woman strengthened her persistence and pressed her request by claiming not to be one of the children, but noting that such a family pet did, in fact, receive crumbs from the table.

The metaphor which Christ had used as a reason for rejecting her petition she turns into a reason for granting it. And He joyfully (if we may venture to say so) allows Himself to be worsted in argument, for He at once accepts her interpretation of the metaphor as proof of her insight and faith. With doglike perseverance, she had excelled even the children in trust, and assuredly she might receive what the children would never miss.[3]

Her great faith was rewarded greatly as Jesus marveled about her and said, "Your request is granted." Matthew relates that from that hour her daughter was healed.

Feeding 4,000 (Matthew 15:29-39)

Verses 29 to 31 summarize Jesus' extensive ministry along the Sea of Galilee and in the mountains of that region. Many infirm and ill people were brought to Jesus to be healed. They responded by praising God. Thus Matthew demonstrates that the ministry of Jesus stayed on target, even though on the previous occasion He was truly excited by the astonishing faith of a Gentile woman.

During this time Jesus again ministered to multitudes of people upon whom He felt compassion. They had been with Him for three days, and He was reluctant to send them on their way without giving them a meal. Once again He appealed to the disciples, who asked where they would get so many loaves in such a desolate place. On this occasion they reported having seven loaves and a few small fish. Jesus went through a similar process of having the multitudes sit and, after offering thanks for the food, gave it to the disciples to dispense.

The people ate to their heart's content and afterward seven large baskets were filled with the leftover loaves and fish. Matthew reports that 4,000 men and a corresponding number of women and children ate this meal.

In this episode some see a redundancy to the previous miraculous feeding found in chapter 14. Nevertheless, clearly these were two distinct occasions, evidenced by several differences. The number fed is reported to be different, the location seems to have changed and the Greek words for the baskets used are different. In the case of the 5,000 who were fed, the baskets were small, pocketbook size baskets, whereas, the baskets used to collect the food after the feeding of the 4,000 were huge baskets. Furthermore, in Matthew 16:9-10 Jesus referred to both feedings as He pressed home a point to the disciples about faith.

After the meal had ended and everyone had eaten to satisfaction, Jesus and the disciples got into a boat and went to the region of Magadan, which is on the east side of the Sea of Galilee.

A Strange Union (Matthew 16:1-12)

At the beginning of chapter 16 we see the Pharisees coming again to an area where, presumably because Jesus was less of a celebrity, they would have greater opportunity to get at Him with their devious motives. Not only was the presence of the fastidious Pharisees at this location highly unusual, but their union with the Sadducees on this occasion was most unorthodox. About all the

Pharisees and Sadducees shared with each other was their Jewish heritage and belief in one god. On the one hand, the Pharisees were a small sect of legalistic, religious fanatics. They trusted not only the written Hebrew Bible but also the oral law and its interpretations handed down over the centuries. They believed in angels and the resurrection. On the other hand, the Sadducees believed in none of these things and accepted only the written books of Scripture, especially the five books of Moses. They were an upper-class, elitist sect, showing allegiance to whatever government would allow them to retain their privileged social position. In many ways they were less of a threat to Jesus than the Pharisees since the Sadducees had little zeal for God and even less influence on the masses.

Seeking again to find fault with Jesus, the Pharisees and Sadducees came to test Him by asking for a "sign from heaven." On the previous occasion (15:1-2) their question was about religious scruples. Now, unashamedly they revealed their motive with a temptation no more disguised than those by the devil in chapter 4. Not content with mere signs upon the earth, such as healing and the multiplying of loaves, the Pharisees and Sadducees asked for a sign "out of the heavens," presumably a voice or perhaps the kind of thing Jesus later predicted would precede the coming of the Son of man (24:29-31).

Mark's Gospel indicates that Jesus sighed deeply in His spirit, demonstrating His grief and lack of patience with this ongoing gamesmanship (Mark 8:12). He replied that although they knew how to interpret signs of the weather, they could not understand "the signs of the times" (Matthew 16:3). The word for "times" here is not the Greek word *chronos*, meaning "literal time," but *kairos*, meaning "right time" or "strategic time."

Since the Pharisees and Sadducees asked for a "sign from heaven," Jesus took the opportunity to point out their inconsistent reasoning. While they accepted the weather patterns as natural phenomena that came from above, they refused to accept Jesus' miracles as anything but natural occurrences. Essentially, He said that they should be less concerned about the origin of the signs and more aware of the meaning of the events surrounding them. Then Jesus repeated what He had told the scribes and Pharisees in 12:39—the only sign they would be given would be the sign of Jonah. Matthew reports that Jesus then left the Pharisees and Sadducees.

Mark's parallel account (Mark 8:10-21) reveals the destination of Jesus. Again, the disciples and Jesus got into a boat to travel across the lake. Mark indicates that enroute Jesus warned the disciples to beware of the leaven of the Pharisees and Sadducees. Unfortunately, the disciples were concerned only about the fact that they had forgotten to bring bread for the journey—a concern that prompted a rebuke from Jesus who called them "men of little faith." He reminded them of both miraculous feedings and of all the leftover food.

Then in verse 11, He reemphasized that He was speaking to them about the leaven of the Pharisees and Sadducees, at which point the disciples understood He was talking about the teachings or doctrines of these groups. Because the doctrines of these two groups differed so widely, most Jews would be tempted to come down on one side or the other. Jesus was telling His disciples to reject the viewpoints of both groups. His use of the word "leaven" to refer to their teachings called attention to the evil and spreading influence of their doctrines.

The Messiah Identified (Matthew 16:13-20)

Wanting again to escape the clamor of the crowds, Jesus and the disciples journeyed to the northern extreme of Palestine to Caesarea Philippi near Mount Hermon, which was the source of the Jordan River about 25 miles north of the Sea of Galilee. Plummer says Jesus wanted "quiet, both from insidious opposition and from noisy popularity."[4]

This setting was the crossroads in the earthly ministry of Jesus as He set out to determine whether His mission of introducing the kingdom of God had been set on an adequate foundation. He began with a general question by asking the disciples who other people claimed Him to be. The responses—John the Baptist, Elijah and Jeremiah—indicated that the public considered Jesus with the highest possible regard. No greater human identification could be sought.

Ultimately, Jesus was not interested in the opinion of the public but in the belief of His intimate followers. Thus He pressed the question, "But what about you? Who do you say I am?" Peter uttered, "You are the Christ, the Son of the living God." With great relief and joy, Jesus pronounced a benediction upon Peter in a very solemn way. In fact, Peter is the only one to whom Jesus uttered the words "blessed are you." Peter was blessed by Jesus not only because he declared the rightful identity of Jesus, but because the heavenly Father was able to use Peter as an agent for revealing truth. Jesus knew that not only would a right understanding of His messiahship be essential for the future ministry of Peter and the other apostles, but also their ability to be channels of God's Word would be equally important.

Verses 18-19 have been the source of much debate, confusion and division in the church. Three questions need explanation: (1) What or who precisely is the "rock" upon which Jesus would build His church? (2) To whom did Jesus give the "keys of the kingdom of heaven" and what are they? and (3) Who received the authority to bind and loose, and what does such authority mean?

The early Christian church had no trouble seeing Peter as its leader. Not only was he a natural leader but he was only the first disciple to declare with conviction that Jesus was the Messiah. This was not the first time Peter had expressed this belief. When his brother Andrew came to him claiming to have found the Messiah, Peter did not

contest that view. He himself had recently declared, "We believe and know that you are the
Holy One of God" (John 6:69). This was a decisive moment, however, because by this time Jesus
had completely shattered the popular notions of a
coming Messiah. Shunning popularity and religious acclaim, living humbly as a man on earth,
clashing so decisively with the religious authorities within Judaism and using His power so discriminately for the advantage of individuals other
than Himself would all be stumbling blocks to belief in His messiahship. Peter and the others had
seen all sides of Jesus and had to combat the popular conceptions about messiahship to come to the
firm conviction that Peter declared here.

Playing on the name Peter, which means a
"stone," Jesus used a metaphor to affirm to Peter
that His church would be built upon a rock so
powerful that the gates of Hades (death) would
not be able to overpower that church. The rock
has historically been identified as either Peter's
apostleship, the truth of Jesus' messiahship or the
act of God revealing His Word through the apostles. The language of these verses do not allow us
to be dogmatic or decisive.[5]

The elevation of the role of Peter and the Roman concept of apostolic succession have motivated Protestant interpreters to try to avoid the
possibility that Jesus was claiming Peter to be the
rock. Furthermore, since Jesus Himself is called
the "cornerstone" (Ephesians 2:20, 1 Peter 2:4-8)
and the apostles and Christian prophets are the

foundation (Ephesians 2:20) it has been argued that Jesus could not have meant for Peter to understand himself to be the rock upon which the church would be built. Nevertheless, that is clearly the most likely and simple explanation of Jesus' words. Quoting Briggs, Plummer notes, "All attempts to explain the 'rock' in any other way than as referring to Peter have ignominiously failed."[6] While neither the confession of Peter nor the faith of Peter may be an adequate explanation of these words, it is clear that the promise is made to Peter upon the confession of his faith.

In all probability Jesus was speaking to Peter as the corporate apostle or as the leader of the Twelve. Jesus took Peter's response to be that of the entire group. While Peter would play the central and most important role in the life of the early church, as attested by Acts 1-10, the ministry of all the apostles in planting the church and communicating divine revelation would be part of that foundation.

The gates of Hades represent the yawning grave that Sadducees viewed as the end of life and Pharisees viewed with great fear, despite their belief in resurrection. The threat of death—the final enemy of mankind—is diffused by the certainty of the building of the church.

Although the Greek word *ekklesia* translated here as "church" is used frequently in the New Testament, we find it only three times in the Gospels—here in Matthew 16:18 and twice in 18:17. Basically, it refers to a body of people united by

common convictions and aims who congregate for
specific purposes. The Roman Senate was spoken
of as an *ekklesia*. The pronoun "my" indicates that
Jesus saw Himself to be the source and owner of
this group, which might also be described as a
New Israel. The precise relation of the church to
the kingdom of God is not always easy to determine. Surely they are not identical. Perhaps it is
too simplistic to say that the church is merely the
earthly expression of the heavenly or spiritual or-
ganism known as the kingdom.

The phrase "keys of the kingdom of heaven"
contrasts with the "gates of Hades." The reason
the gates of Hades would not have power to overcome the church of Christ is that the power of the
kingdom of heaven is available through the use of
these special keys. That authority is expressed in
the concept of binding and loosing. Jesus was not
referring here to the binding and loosing of sins in
condemnation or absolution. Rather, the thought
is that Peter and the apostles were given authority
to "forbid and permit." As leaders of the church
they would be put into a position to make decisions about orthodoxy based on their historical
and organic connectedness to Jesus. This is why,
according to Acts 1:21-22, apostleship was limited
to those who had accompanied Jesus on earth and
had been witnesses to His resurrection.

The so-called messianic secret, usually identified with Mark's Gospel, is declared nowhere
more clearly than here in Matthew 16:20. Earlier
many who had been healed were warned not to

spread the news of Jesus' identity. Now the disciples, who have a clear understanding of who He is, are warned not to divulge it to others.

Death Predicted (Matthew 16:21-23)

Now that His messianic identity was clearly known by the disciples, Jesus "began to explain to his disciples that he must go to Jerusalem and suffer many things at the hands of the elders, chief priests and teachers of the law, and that he must be killed and on the third day be raised to life" (16:21). The word "began" implies the continuing of a process which we know proceeded even into the Last Supper (Matthew 26:31). The three perpetrators of the suffering and death of Jesus are identified as the elders, chief priests and scribes who were, in fact, the three groups that comprised the Sanhedrin. Peter and the other apostles had seen Jesus frequently clash with these respective religious groups, but the thought that these religious controversies could result in such a tragedy as the death of their newly acclaimed Messiah was beyond Peter's ability to accept. His reaction, presumably representative of the Twelve, indicates that their understanding of messiahship was still far from accurate. Usurping Jesus' leadership, Peter took Him aside to counsel Him, much as a mentor would guide an apprentice. In typical fashion, Peter made a rash and bold statement, invoking God's name and saying this would never happen to Jesus. This is an early hint of Peter's bravado in which perhaps he was even insisting that he would be the bodyguard of Jesus so that such a tragedy could not occur. Without any doubt, Peter's motivation was love, albeit misguided love.

> Peter's primacy is of a strangely varied character, and it is sometimes a primacy of evil rather than of good. If he is first in rank, and first in confession of faith, he is also first in tempting, and first in denying, his Master. The rock of foundation almost at once becomes a rock of offense, and that, not to the Church, but to its very Builder.[7]

Jesus' response, "Get behind me, Satan!" may seem to be disproportionate to the offense. The mention of Satan, which means "adversary," recalls the temptation narrative in Matthew 4 where early in His ministry Jesus was tempted to be diverted from the way of the cross. Peter, who had recently been acclaimed to be a rock and a foundation stone to the church, now is called a stumbling block. This is the same term Peter used earlier (15:12) to tell Jesus that the Pharisees were "offended" about the accusations of Jesus. Now Jesus uses the word to tell Peter that he is trying to "trip up" Jesus, and that is offensive to Him. The severity of the rebuke is more readily understood as Jesus explained that Peter was setting his mind not on God's interests but on human interests.

The suffering He would undergo would severely test the will of Jesus, as we will see in the prayer of agony in the Garden of Gethsemane. Jesus needed the support of His immediate followers rather than the eroding influence of their consorting with Satan to divert Jesus from His mission. Considering the high stakes, the rebuke certainly was not too harsh.

Discipleship Demands (Matthew 16:24-28)

Seizing this sobering moment, Jesus went on to tell His followers what discipleship would mean. If messiahship meant suffering and death, discipleship would also have a cost. Jesus was throwing down the gauntlet here, putting the decision to follow Him into the hands of the disciples. The "if" clause indicates that Jesus was giving them the choice. Some might wish to come after Him (16:24). Others might wish to save their own life (16:25). In each case an inevitable consequence would follow. In the former, they must deny themselves and take up their cross and follow Jesus. In the latter, the consequence of wishing to save one's life was to lose it. This "pay me now or pay me later" formula gave the disciples a measure of freedom but also assured them of the inescapable consequences of their choices. Just in case they were thinking it might be more advantageous to avoid the way of suffering, Jesus reinforced the idea that whoever would try to maintain his own life would lose it, because no matter how much they would gain, they would in the final analysis be losers. The temporary rewards of the world pale in comparison to the advantage of gaining eternal life.

The ideas of Jesus' suffering and dying and of disciples having to deny themselves and take up their own cross to follow Jesus apparently blocked any recognition that Jesus claimed (16:21) that He would be raised on a third day. The end of all the suffering would redeem the situation and make the temporary inconveniences quite worthy of the permanent improvements. To assure them, Jesus said that the Son of Man would return "in his Father's glory with his angels" (16:27). That coming of the Son of man would be more in line with the messianic expectations prevailing in the current Jewish thought. He would come as the omnipotent Judge, not as a mere human.

The thought of the end times led Jesus to predict the event that would pull the curtains back, so to speak, on the heavenly kingdom. Mark and Luke use different terminology than Matthew by saying that some who were present would not experience death "before they see the kingdom of God," which likely refers to the transfiguration that occurs as the next event in all three synoptic Gospels. Matthew amplifies the idea by saying that those who participated in this experience would actually see the Son of Man coming in His kingdom, showing His more central role in the experience.

Some who have understood Matthew 16:28 to refer to the second advent are contradicted by history. The phrasing of that verse is so specific that it can mean nothing other than that some who were literally and physically standing in the presence of Jesus at the moment He uttered His statement would also before their death see the Son of Man coming in His kingdom. None of the apostles have survived the nearly 2,000 years since this declaration, nor has the second advent occurred. We are justified, therefore, in seeing 16:28 as a reference to the transfiguration. In fact, Matthew, whose order of events often varies from that of Mark and Luke, follows them precisely at this point, thus indicating his understanding of the statement of Jesus also to be referring to the transfiguration. Other scholars, such as Barclay, see this promise as a reference to Pentecost and the subsequent events when the power of the kingdom would be more publicly visible. However, the context argues strongly for the interpretation we have given.

The Transfiguration (Matthew 17:1-13)

Fourteen miles north of Caesarea Philippi stands the lofty Mount Hermon, about 9,400 feet high. No doubt this was the sight of the transfiguration reported in Matthew 17, Mark 9 and Luke 9. The three accounts agree in details with minor differences that are easily explainable. With Him, Jesus took Peter, James and John to go up the mountain to pray. While He was praying (Luke 9:29) the appearance of Jesus changed, His face shining brightly and His garments becoming as white as light. Moses and Elijah also appeared in a glorious fashion, and they were talking to Jesus about His departure (the Greek word is *exodus*), which Jesus would accomplish at Jerusalem.

We might ask why these two men in particular of all of the Old Testament heroes would appear with Jesus. Two suggestions have been put forward. First, both Moses and Elijah ended their time on earth in a rather irregular way. Moses went on the mountain to die alone, and the text says that God buried him there. In point of fact, no human being witnessed Moses' death. Elijah was taken by God in a fiery chariot and escaped the earthly death experience. Jewish thought frequently pointed to the expectation that Elijah would return as a forerunner of the Messiah, and some Jewish literature had the expectation that Moses would accompany the Messiah.

Second, these two appeared because they are the primary representatives of the law and the prophets. Moses was the lawgiver and Elijah was always considered to be the greatest of the prophets. The message for the disciples was clear: As great as the law and prophets were, the representative of the gospel is far greater.

Two testimonies to the superiority of Jesus were forthcoming. A voice from the cloud said, "This is my Son, whom I love; with him I am well pleased. Listen to him!" We may reasonably assume that a strong emphasis was put on the word "him." In other words, although the law, prophets and gospel were represented, the voice from the cloud said that the gospel had supremacy. Furthermore, when the cloud lifted and the glory departed, the disciples lifted their eyes and saw only Jesus. The other two disappeared from the vision while Jesus remained to accomplish the work of God.

No doubt this experience was a great consolation to the disciples who were still reeling from the thought that their newly acclaimed Messiah was going to suffer and die. Also, they were perhaps still stung by the harsh rebuke Jesus gave to Peter. Now they are assured that even though such suffering lies ahead, the Messiah has not been rejected by God and the end of the road is filled with glory. Perhaps even for Jesus this was a moment of reassurance that as He continued to travel toward the cross He would not be alone. Although all the apostles would abandon Him, clearly this experience strengthened Him.

Perhaps because this vision was so comforting, Peter boldly requested that they prolong the event by building three tabernacles or sacred booths, one for each of the three transfigured persons. Mark mentions that Peter spoke up on behalf of the others because all three of them were a bit perplexed by this episode and did not know what to say. While Peter was making this suggestion, a cloud of glory overshadowed all of them and the voice of God came out of the cloud. Perhaps the cloud was the famous Shekinah glory that appeared in the exodus and remained with the ark of the covenant. No doubt for Jesus great comfort came from hearing the same affirmation of His being the Beloved Son as He heard after His baptism (Matthew 3:17, KJV). The response of the disciples to the voice was typical of all such theophanies. They fell on their faces (17:6). Although Jesus told the three not to report this episode until after He had risen from the dead, the impact of this event on Peter is evident in Second Peter 1:16-18.

Now fully convinced of His messiahship, the disciples turned to the doctrinal question that any Jew would ask, namely, how could the Messiah come without Elijah coming first to restore all things as had been prophesied in Malachi 4:5? Jesus then explained to them that Elijah had already come, which the disciples understood as being fulfilled in the person of John the Baptist.

The Demoniac Boy (Matthew 17:14-23)

As so often happens, this moment of great glory was followed immediately by an earthly challenge. As the four descended the mountain, they came upon a multitude out of which came forth one man who, falling on his knees before Jesus, begged for mercy for his son whom Mark and Luke describe as being demon possessed, but whom Matthew describes as being a lunatic or epileptic (the Greek word literally means "moon struck," and appears in the New Testament only here and Matthew 4:24). As verse 18 indicates, Matthew agrees with the diagnosis of the boy being demonized. The nine disciples who did not ascend the mountain were unable to effect a cure of the young man, which was a source of exaspera-

tion to Jesus. In fact, rebounding from the beauty
of the transfiguration, Jesus seems all the more
eager to be done with the earthly experience with
its severe limitations (17:17). Whether the "unbelieving and perverse generation" refers to the failure of the apostles and their weakness or to the
entire society around Him is unclear.

With one word of rebuke, Jesus exorcised the
demon who left the boy. According to Mark, the
healing took place in two stages because the boy
appeared like a corpse after the exorcism so that
many claimed he was dead. Jesus, however, took
the lad by the hand and raised him up to full
health and life. The disciples, who found themselves publicly humiliated and disappointed with
their inability to effect a miracle, asked Jesus pri-
vately why they could not cast out the demon. Jesus replied that it was their lack of faith that
prohibited them from being effective. Then He
told them that faith as small as a mustard seed
would be powerful enough to move a mountain.[8]
This metaphorical expression was a common one
in Judaism and certainly was not meant to be
taken literally. Plummer notes that Jesus assured
the disciples that the fault lay in themselves because He had earlier given them power that they
had used effectively to cast out demons.

> Unconsciously they had fallen away into a
> condition of mind in which they trusted
> either too much in themselves, as if the
> power were their own; or too little in Christ,

as if in this difficult case He might fail
them.[9]

From the north country the disciples and Jesus
returned to Galilee where again Jesus declared
that He was going to be killed and raised on the
third day. At this point the disciples understood
Jesus better and "were filled with grief" (17:23).
Unfortunately, they still did not understand the
prediction of the resurrection which, in fact, they
never did understand until after He had risen.
This is a crucial point for rebuffing those who
deny the reality of the resurrection based on an al-
leged plot by the disciples to make it appear so.
Far from trying to stage this event, the idea of resurrection never entered their minds, even though
Jesus predicted it on several occasions.

Paying Taxes (Matthew 17:24-27)

When they returned to Capernaum on the
north shore of the Sea of Galilee (Peter's and Jesus' adopted hometown), Peter was confronted by
tax collectors from the temple who asked whether
or not Jesus conformed to Jewish practice by paying the two-drachma tax, an equivalent of two
days pay. This annual tax to sustain the operation
of the temple in Jerusalem was prescribed in Exodus 30:13. Peter's quick assurance that Jesus
would pay the tax gives evidence of his growing
understanding of Jesus and his growing confidence as a leader.

The next two incidents demonstrate the divine

foreknowledge that Jesus wants Peter to understand. First, before Peter uttered a word about the tax, Jesus preempted him by telling a short parable relevant to the situation. Then, by telling Peter to catch a fish that would contain the coin, Jesus also highlighted that divine foreknowledge.

The parable Jesus told implies that Jesus considered Himself to be legitimately exempt from paying the tax. Because His Father was the owner of the temple (see Luke 2:49), Jesus as the Son should not have to pay the tax. Nevertheless, to avoid causing someone to stumble over the example of Jesus in not paying, He chose to conform to the practice. The word translated "offend" in 17:27 is the Greek word *skandalizo* (also found in 15:12; 18:6, 8, 9), which literally means "cause to be caught, to fall or give offense to." Jesus was teaching the disciples here that despite their freedom as sons of the kingdom, they would need to impose certain restrictions upon themselves for the effectiveness of their ministry.

The miracle of this story lies solely in Jesus knowing beforehand that the first fish Peter would catch would have the required coin. The fact that a fish might have swallowed a coin was not necessarily supernatural but Jesus' knowledge of it certainly was. Some commentators have interpreted this event metaphorically, noting that for Jesus to use His miraculous power in this way would be uncharacteristic of Him. On many occasions, starting with the temptation events in Matthew 4, Jesus declined opportunities to use His

power for personal advantage. Furthermore, it is
claimed that Jesus would be setting a poor example for His followers by encouraging laziness,
which also seems to be uncharacteristic of Jesus.
Even Plummer states, "But we may allow the possibility of metaphor, or of the exact words used by
Christ being either misunderstood or modified in
tradition. 'In the fish that thou shalt catch thou
shalt find what will pay for Me and for thee'
might mean that the fish would sell for as much;
and this would easily take the form which Mt. records."[10] In other words, Peter would catch a fish,
sell it and use the earnings to pay the tax.

This overcomes the difficulties noted above but
poses even more severe difficulties. If Jesus had
intended for Peter merely to catch a fish to pay
the tax, He would not have invented the idea
about finding a coin in the fish's mouth. Although
He used metaphors from time to time, Jesus
would not have wanted His disciples or anyone
else to misunderstand such an important concept
as His use of His miraculous power. Furthermore,
had this episode been devoid of any miraculous
element, there would have been no reason for
Matthew to record such a natural and common incident. Also, it is doubtful that one fish could have
been sold for the equivalent of two days' wages.

Clearly it is preferable to understand that teaching Peter and the disciples the important lesson of
His divine foreknowledge was an overriding concern that motivated Jesus to use His power in this
way. Furthermore, because He was the Son of the

Owner of the temple and also the Son of the Owner of the sea, it was clearly the prerogative of Jesus to draw a coin out of a fish's mouth to pay the temple tax. Reasserting His identity in such a dramatic way was more important at this point than being misjudged about His use of power.

Summary of Major Themes

This lesson in faith is the last of six such important episodes in this section that teach the disciples about faith. We recall the miracles of the loaves and fish being multiplied on two occasions (14:13-20; 15:32-39), which were to be understood as lessons in faith (16:8). Peter's effort to emulate Jesus by walking on water resulted in a lesson of faith (14:31). The great faith of the Canaanite woman was rewarded by the healing of her daughter (15:28). The expulsion of the demon from the young lad was not accomplished by the disciples because of the littleness of their faith (17:20).

Another important theme in this narrative section is how Jesus helped the disciples to gain a kingdom mentality. On three occasions they had seen supernatural provision of their needs: the two miraculous feedings and the coin for the temple tax. They also saw Jesus challenging religious traditions that interfered with moral obligations (15:1-14). They learned much about messiahship: In Caesarea Philippi, Peter recognized Jesus as the Messiah; Peter, James and John had that truth affirmed on the Mount of Transfiguration. Also, on three occasions they heard Jesus predict that He would suffer and die (16:23; 17:12 and 17:22-23). They were offended and grieved about this prospect and probably horrified at the determination of Jesus to follow through with this plan.

Finally in this section, we see Matthew's emphasis on the primacy of Peter. It was Peter who walked on the water, who asked for an explanation of the parable about food not defiling a person, who confessed Jesus to be the Messiah, who rebuked Jesus and in return was rebuked by Jesus, who was one of the three at the transfiguration and who was responsible to catch the fish to pay the temple tax.

Thus, through 16 episodes in this important narrative section, Matthew presents an emphasis on discipleship, including faith in particular; an understanding about kingdom mentality, including the implications of messiahship; and a focus on the foremost among the apostles, namely, Peter.

Endnotes

1. Alfred Plummer, *An Exegetical Commentary on The Gospel According to St. Matthew* (Grand Rapids: Baker Book House, 1982), p. 205.
2. Ibid., p. 206.
3. Ibid., p. 217.
4. Ibid., p. 214.
5. Some have seen a distinction between *petros*, Peter's name, and *petra*, meaning "rock." The change of gender in Greek conforms only to natural language usage. In any case, Jesus was

speaking in Aramaic and would have used the word *kepha* in both instances.

6. Plummer, p. 229.
7. Ibid., p. 234.
8. Verse 21, "but this kind does not go out except by prayer and fasting," lacks good manuscript evidence in Matthew but the same idea is expressed in Mark 9:29, which has better manuscript support.
9. Plummer, p. 242.
10. Ibid., p. 247.

CHAPTER 8

Discipline in the Kingdom

Matthew 18

The fourth discourse in Matthew's Gospel consists of one chapter and contains two emphases: forgiveness and discipline. Maybe it was the privileged status of Peter, James and John who attended the transfiguration while the other disciples experienced frustrating failure with the demonized boy (17:16); or maybe it was Peter's elevated status in representing the rest of the disciples to the temple tax collector; or maybe it was Jesus' latest prediction about His death and resurrection (John 9:31). Whatever it was, something caused the disciples to begin talking about who would be greatest in the kingdom of heaven.

We know that the disciples were not above petty arguments. Both Mark (9:33-37) and Luke (9:46-48; see also 22:24) poignantly reported details of such an incident, whereas Matthew (18:1) seems to protect the apostles by omitting the details. In Matthew's account the issue seems to be

more theoretical and theological than personal.
The question, "Who is the greatest in the kingdom
of heaven?" could be taken to be merely the kind
of intellectual intrigue enjoyed so much by the
Jewish mind. Jesus, however, took the occasion as
an opportunity to teach the disciples the nature of
kingdom greatness.

Calling a child into their midst, Jesus told the
disciples how far off track they were; they would
need to turn around completely. The word change
(*be converted*, KJV) translates the Greek word *stre-
pho*, which means "to turn, change inwardly."
Rather than striving for adult sophistication and
greatness, kingdom stature demands childlikeness.
In fact, entry to the kingdom itself requires that
one become like a child.

What qualities or characteristics of a child
might Jesus have had in mind specifically? Barclay
suggests humility, dependency and trust, whereas
Plummer speaks about the "childlike attitude,
which does not seek prominence but shrinks from
it."[1] The humility Jesus spoke about in verse 4 is
the humility that does not demand self-attention.
While children demand much attention to their
personal needs, they do not seek public acclaim or
stature, which is what concerned the disciples. To
emphasize the importance of childlikeness for
kingdom entry, Jesus said that a disciple who received or welcomed a child would indeed be receiving Jesus Himself (v. 5). Doing this "in my
name" refers to doing it for the sake of Jesus, or
pronouncing the blessing of Jesus upon such a

child. Receiving the child may refer either to the act of welcoming a child or a childlike person, or seeing Christ in the child and embracing the child because of Christ.

A Strong Warning (Matthew 18:6-9)

The converse of welcoming a child is stated in the strongest of terms. By His own example in dealing with the poll tax issue, Jesus had just shown how important it is not to give offense or cause others to stumble. The spirit of pride and independence that Jesus might have exhibited on that earlier occasion might cause one of these "little ones" to stumble. Jesus warned that it would be far better to be attached to a heavy millstone and be thrown into the sea to drown than to be guilty of causing a little one to sin. The millstone Jesus referred to was a huge stone used in grinding grain. Perhaps it is not coincidental that Jesus referred to this form of execution as an example of penalty for one who interferes with a member of His kingdom. Barclay notes, "The Jews took the view that the most unforgivable of all sins is to teach another to sin. . . ."[2] The Romans used this form of execution for political criminals, but Jews viewed it as being excessively inhumane and therefore avoided it. Jewish people in general had a great dread of the sea, so Jesus chose perhaps the most extreme example imaginable to illustrate the importance of not causing a little one to stumble.

The little ones may literally refer to children, or to childlike people who are fresh in faith and innocence. Causing others to stumble is the very work of hell, as we have already seen when Jesus accused Peter of being a stumbling block to Him and called Peter by the name "Satan" (16:23). Fortunately for Peter, Jesus certainly was not one of the little ones, so the millstone idea would not apply to him.

The Greek word *skandalon* primarily means a "trap," and in Matthew 18:7 it carries the sense of "something that causes someone to sin." Scripture mentions three ways people set such traps. Romans 14:13-17 indicates that abusing Christian liberty may cause a weaker Christian to stumble. *Skandalon* also occurs in Romans 16:17 ("obstacles," NIV; "hindrances," NASB), where it refers to doctrinally incorrect teaching that sets a trap. John assured his readers that if they love one another they will not cause anyone to stumble (1 John 2:10). The converse would indicate that not loving a fellow Christian may be a cause of stumbling to that person.

Moving from the idea of causing a child to stumble to the idea of stumbling blocks to our own spiritual well-being, Jesus warned the disciples with some extreme illustrations. Noting the inevitability of stumbling blocks (Matthew 18:7), Jesus pronounced a woe on the causes of those stumbling blocks. Sometimes those causes are within ourselves. Verses 8 and 9 say that it is better for one to amputate a hand or foot or to pluck out an eye, if those members cause one to sin, than to remain whole but be a source of stumbling to someone else.

These verses parallel others we have already studied in the Sermon on the Mount (5:29-30). Our comments there will suffice for an understanding of these verses, except to note that again Jesus affirms His conviction about the reality of a fiery hell.

While there is no question that Jesus believed in the reality and literal existence of hell, it is clear that the idea of removing a hand, foot or eye is to be taken metaphorically. Repeatedly Jesus taught the disciples that it is one's inward disposition, or heart, that causes a person to sin. One less hand or foot does not make an amputee less inclined to sin. It is unlikely that Jesus was talking about mutilation of one's body as a source for finding spiritual purity. Rather, He was saying it would be better for a person to be physically maimed in heaven than to find oneself to be totally healthy in hell.

The Lost Sheep (Matthew 18:10-14)

Verse 10 recaptures the thought about not abusing little ones. It states that disciples should not despise even one little one because their guardian angels are close to God in heaven. The word "see" is the same word Jesus used in 16:6 to warn the disciples to beware of the Pharisees, which indicates the importance of the command. Verse 11 has weak manuscript evidence, although the same uncontested words are found in Luke 19:10.

Not content merely to warn the disciples about the seriousness of causing a little one to stumble,

Jesus continued to extol the importance of children by telling a brief parable. Although this parable is more beautifully related in Luke 15:4-7, the point comes across adequately here that the value of an individual is so great that risking the 99 is appropriate. The connection is well stated by Plummer: "If God takes so much trouble to recover a little one that has strayed, how grievous it must be to cause it to stray. Rather, every effort should be made to prevent it from straying."[3] God's affection for the little ones is so great that it is His will that not one of them should perish. Notice that, "my Father" of verse 10 has become "your Father" in verse 14. The disciples are thus encouraged to obey, not simply out of duty to Jesus' Father but out of affection for their own heavenly Father.

Discipline in the Church (Matthew 18:15-20)

The transition to the next section of discourse is easily made. Plummer says, "The way in which God deals with His erring sheep leads on to the way in which a man should deal with his erring brother. He should endeavor to seek and recover him who has gone astray."[4]

Verses 15-20 of Matthew 18 are frequently appealed to in matters of church discipline, and rightly so. Although the Christian church was not yet established and would not be until after Pentecost, Jesus uses the word "church" for the third time in this Gospel (twice in 18:17; see also 16:18). The word *ekklesia* means a body summoned to-

gether or a congregation. If Jesus was prescribing
a formula for immediate reconciling within a formal group, He must have been referring to a Jewish assembly, perhaps the synagogue. This would
not be inconsistent with His view of the synagogue. The focus of this section, however, is not
on church government but on brotherly reconciliation. Perhaps going back to verse 7 and the subject of stumbling blocks, Jesus now endeavored to
help His disciples learn how to handle sins that
had been committed against each other. A textual
variation leaves it unclear as to whether the prescription is given in a case of a brother who sins or
a brother who sins "against you." Since there is no
other synoptic parallel to this text, we must com-
pare it with other ideas in Scripture to determine
whether Jesus was prescribing that a disciple
should reprove a brother who had sinned against
him personally or one who had sinned in general.
Luke 17:3 would argue for the latter; the sin need
not be committed personally against one in order
to reprove it. Similarly, the Pauline injunction in
Galatians 6:1 would imply the broader responsibility.

We need to emphasize that the purpose for discipline is restoration, not merely punishment or
public humiliation. The initial act of reproving the
sinner needs to be done in private. The hope
should be that the brother will listen to the one reproving and the relationship will be restored with
no further action required.

In the event, however, that the sinning brother

refuses to listen, the reprover is told to take one or two others with him for a second confrontation. This is in obedience to the prescription given in Deuteronomy 19:15. The witnesses need not have personally witnessed the sin but are witnesses to the fact that the reprover is genuinely seeking to achieve reconciliation. Prior to exposing the sinner to any more than one or two witnesses, every attempt needs to be made to achieve reconciliation in the most amicable way possible. The witnesses are not necessarily advocates of the one doing the reproving, but are present to ensure proper attitudes and fair treatment. If, in fact, they find that the erring brother needs to be reproved, perhaps they will be able to help persuade him.

If this attempt fails, the wronged person is to "tell it to the church." It is assumed that the erring brother is a brother also to those who are in the church and that those members will care about this reconciliation as much as the one who is wronged. As a congregation, they have the responsibility to hear the case of the one who was wronged, as well as the evidence brought by the witnesses that every effort has been made to achieve reconciliation. Even after such testimony has come forth, the congregation has a responsibility to render a fair judgment. If the erring brother is, indeed, deemed as being in the wrong, the church then makes an appeal to him. The church ought to use as a last resort its authority to remove the brother from their membership. But if the erring brother refuses to listen even to the church, then he is to be regarded as "a pagan or a tax collector" (18:17).

We might automatically assume that this means that the erring brother is to be excommunicated. The notorious example of the young man living illicitly with his stepmother, described in First Corinthians 5, is often cited as an example of the proper way to handle church discipline of this nature. The apostle Paul insisted that the young man be removed from the assembly (1 Corinthians 5:13). This stratagem seemed to be effective; the young man repented and was restored to church membership (2 Corinthians 2:5-8). The usual interpretation is that this illustration perfectly describes the intention of the church discipline that was prescribed by Jesus in Matthew 18. And this interpretation is most likely correct.

Nevertheless, we must honestly note that Matthew 18 says nothing specifically about excommunicating the offending brother. We may make the assumption that being treated as a pagan and a tax collector warranted such excommunication. On the other hand, we have seen how Jesus Himself treated Gentiles and tax collectors. In the case of Gentiles, while He came not specifically to minister to them, when they pressed their claim He responded to their need with compassion (recall Matthew 15:21-28, the Canaanite woman). In the case of tax collectors, Jesus consistently ministered with compassion to such as Levi (Matthew 9:9) and Zacchaeus (Luke 19:1-10). Also, recall that Jesus was

called "the friend of tax collectors and 'sinners' "
(Matthew 11:19). In fact, Jesus even stated that tax
collectors and harlots will get into the kingdom of
God before the scribes and Pharisees (Matthew
21:31). In other words, rather than excommunicating the offending brother, Jesus may be calling on
the church to have a forbearing spirit and persist in
ministering to those who seem to be most unyield-
ing and challenging.

Knowing that church discipline puts many
Christians outside their comfort zone and may require some believers to work contrary to their
more compassionate nature, Jesus assured the disciples of their authority in these matters by making available to them the power to bind and loose
that He had given to Peter (see 16:19). While some
commentators believe that verses 17-20 are frag-
mentary sayings that have been grouped together
by Matthew, no textual evidence warrants that
conclusion. At first glance it may appear that the
disciples, when they are gathered as the church,
have authority to forgive or condemn on earth and
that whatever they choose to do would be ratified
in heaven; furthermore, the heavenly Father is ob-
ligated to act on the agreement of any two disciples in matters of church discipline. Some
segments of the church have assumed this to be
the proper interpretation and have also assumed
this kind of authority.

Another approach to understanding these
verses, which is more consistent with the rest of
Scripture, is to consider first the idea in verse 20

where Jesus assured the disciples that when they are gathered, even in a group as small as two or three, He is in their presence. With that in mind as well the implication that He exercises leadership wherever He is present, we may well assume that their binding and loosing will be under His authority and will be sanctioned in heaven. Jesus is hereby giving the disciples confidence that He will take leadership in guiding them, even when only two of them need to make major decisions for the church.

Forgiveness and Mercy (Matthew 18:21-35)

Peter may not have been keeping up with Jesus in this discourse. When he finally got a chance to ask a question, he leap-frogged back to verse 15 where Jesus had spoken about a brother sinning against another brother. Undoubtedly, the rest of the teaching on church discipline would be important for Peter at some time in his life, but for the moment, he dwelt upon the responsibility of forgiving another brother. Did he have someone specific in mind? We do not know. Nevertheless, knowing the compassionate nature of Jesus, Peter undoubtedly felt extremely generous by offering to forgive someone up to seven times.

Jewish tradition limited the necessity to forgive to three times. Amos 1:3, 6, 9 and Job 33:29 were used to justify this limit. Peter's focus, however, was on the rights of the one being wronged rather than on the restoration of the erring brother. Also, he did not seem to understand Jesus' point of view, namely, when an offense has been forgiven, it is canceled.

To illustrate the point, Jesus told a powerful and clear parable. The contrast presented between the forgiving, merciful king and the unforgiving, unmerciful slave could not be greater. Notice that this is another kingdom parable: "The kingdom of heaven is like . . ." (Matthew 18:23). The reference to settling accounts in verse 23 anticipates the idea of a final reckoning at judgment day.

In the parable a slave owing 10,000 talents (comparable to over 10 million dollars) was brought to the king. This huge debt could only be incurred by someone in a very responsible position who must have embezzled huge amounts collected for the king. Such criminal activity would merit the harshest of punishment, which is indicated in verse 25. Realizing his plight, the servant prostrated himself before the king, asking for patience and promising to repay the entire debt—a promise that both he and the king knew would be impossible to fulfill.

Nevertheless, the master had pity on him and released him and forgave him the entire debt. We should note here that the word for "forgave" in verse 27 is the word used by Jesus in verse 18, translated "loose." In other words, having given the church authority to loose or release people, Jesus then illustrated the limitless forgiveness that God expects His people to express.

The parable might well end here and the point be made sufficiently for Peter to understand the importance of forgiving an offending brother. But Jesus continued the story by saying that the newly forgiven man sought out a fellow servant who owed him 100 denarii (equivalent to three or four months of wages). The text suggests some violence, as the forgiven man seized and began to choke the indebted one, insisting that he pay back immediately what was owed. The indebted servant prostrated himself before his creditor and begged for patience in almost the exact same terms used earlier by the first servant who requested mercy from the king. Unfortunately, the forgiven man did not show the grace or mercy shown by the king. Rather, he threw his debtor into prison, which was his legal right. Fellow servants, seeing what had happened, reported to the king the harsh treatment by the one man against the other. The angered king brought in the "wicked servant" to call him to account. The king naturally expected that his forgiven servant would have shown the same mercy he had received. In response, the king handed him over to jailers who detained him until his entire debt was paid. Jesus summarized the parable in verse 35: "This is how my heavenly Father will treat each of you unless you forgive your brother from your heart."

A legal expert might object to the events of this parable by saying each person has the prerogative of showing mercy or requiring the demands of the law. If the king chose to forgive, that was his choice and his business. The servant who received forgiveness, while perhaps being morally obliged to grant such mercy, was not legally required to do so and acted perfectly within his own rights. But that misses the entire point of the parable, which expresses the economy of the kingdom of heaven (18:23). The nature of the kingdom is to act on behalf of the welfare of others and not insist on one's own, self-centered rights. Plummer states it this way: "An unforgiving spirit is sure to provoke the anger of God; so much so, that His free forgiveness of sinners ceases to flow to them, when in this way they offend. So to speak, it revives the guilt of their otherwise forgiven sins."[5] The commentator goes on to express gratitude that Matthew preserved this parable for us, "For we are not apt to think of what seems to be a merely negative quality,—the absence of a forgiving temper, as a fatal sin."[6]

No response of the disciples is noted by Matthew. While this teaching must have been received as a radical idea, we should recall that it was not entirely new to them (see, for example, 5:23-26 and 6:14-15). It was also a teaching they would receive near the end of Holy Week (see Mark 11:25).

What may seem most surprising in this teaching is the conditional nature of God's mercy. He who shows no mercy loses the mercy that he has been shown. Other Scripture also confirms this idea: "Judgment without mercy will be shown to anyone who has not been merciful" (James 2:13).

The challenge given by Jesus in Matthew 18:35 is surprisingly direct. While addressing the disciples, Jesus uses "you" and "your" four times in one verse to refer to the disciples. Jesus clearly intended for them to understand that although they had been given the power to bind and loose, the spirit and nature of the kingdom required them to be quick to forgive because they themselves had been forgiven much. Like the one who escaped the sheepfold and was retrieved out on the mountain at the risk of the other 99, and like the children in the kingdom whose value to the heavenly Father is so evident, so, too, must the errant brother be treated with the greatest possible compassion and conciliation. Far from establishing a simple legalistic formula for local church polity, Matthew 18 prescribes a principle requiring people of the kingdom to exhibit the character of the king.

Endnotes

1. Alfred Plummer, *An Exegetical Commentary on The Gospel According to St. Matthew* (Grand Rapids: Baker Book House, 1982), p. 249.
2. William Barclay, *The Gospel of Matthew*, Vol. 2 (Philadelphia: The Westminster Press, 1958), p. 197.
3. Plummer, p. 252.
4. Ibid., p. 252-253.
5. Ibid., p. 257.
6. Ibid.

CHAPTER 9

Kingdom Citizenship

Matthew 19-22

The fifth narrative section of Matthew's Gospel predictably begins with an end-of-discourse formula: "When Jesus had finished saying these things . . ." (Matthew 19:1). Having imparted lessons on humility and forgiveness to His disciples, Jesus was now about to embark on the final stage of His earthly mission. Leaving Galilee and moving toward the region of Judea, Jesus continued purposefully toward His destiny. Meanwhile, great multitudes were continuing to follow Him as He continued His ministry of teaching and healing.

The four chapters that comprise this narrative section contain 18 sections, which primarily develop three themes: discipleship training, kingdom citizenship and conflict. Nine of the sections actually contain two of these themes. The theme of discipleship training runs through chapters 19 and 20, with some overlap of kingdom citizenship.

The theme of conflict runs throughout chapters 21 and 22, with some overlap of kingdom citizenship.

Divorce (Matthew 19:3-12)

Having encountered the Pharisees in places far away from Judea to the north and the east, Jesus might rightly have assumed that as He approached Judea He would be even more the object of their scrutiny. Not missing a trick, the Pharisees, already knowing that Jesus condemned divorce (5:31-32) saw a way to put Jesus in opposition with the Mosaic law that allowed for divorce (Deuteronomy 24:1). The question they posed was whether it was lawful for a man to divorce his wife for any reason at all. Almost all Jews believed that divorce was allowed, but there was sharp debate about what constituted legitimate grounds for divorce. Two rabbis from earlier centuries taught opposing views. The school of Rabbi Hillel held to a loose interpretation of Deuteronomy 24:1, while the school of Rabbi Shammai held to the view that only for the reason of infidelity would a man be allowed to put away his wife. The controversy centered on the Deuteronomic phrase, "if she finds no favor in his eyes" (KJV). In such an instance the husband was allowed to write a certificate of divorce and send his wife away.

Jesus bypassed the debate but clung to the conservative principle emphasizing the original purpose of marriage found in Genesis 1:27 and 2:24.

The principle was this: In the beginning God made one male and one female and intended them to remain together in an intimate relationship. The intimacy of future marriage relationships was to be so great that they transcended the parent-child relationship, resulting in a new unity of flesh. The conclusive argument in Jesus' response was, "Therefore what God has joined together, let man not separate." The focus here is on the fact that marriage is God's plan, and when divorce occurs God is not a party to it.

Not content with this response, or the fact that Jesus too easily eluded their treachery, the Pharisees contrasted this view with the "command" of Moses that specified that a husband should give the wife a bill of divorce. Jesus easily cut through their reasoning by showing that Moses did not command divorce, but allowed for it because of the hard-heartedness of men. He insisted again that the principles for marriage and divorce do not go back merely to Moses but back to the very beginning. Then He came down squarely on the side of the conservative school of thought by saying that "anyone who divorces his wife, except for marital unfaithfulness, and marries another woman commits adultery" (Matthew 19:9). In other words, the divorce was not legitimate in the eyes of God; therefore, the man who was on his second marriage was living illegitimately with another woman.

The Pharisees clearly did not achieve their purpose and withdrew from Jesus. But the issue was not entirely settled in the minds of the disciples. Seeing how intensely Jesus held to the principle of no divorce, the disciples wondered aloud whether it would be more reasonable for a man not to marry than to enter a relationship from which they could not separate themselves. Jesus responded saying that not everyone would be able to accept the celibate life because the desirability of marriage was so strong that most men would enter that relationship despite the possible negative consequences. Those who could accept celibacy, however, are divided into three categories: (1) some were born as eunuchs; (2) others were made eunuchs for the sake of their service to an emperor or other leader who required that his servants not be a threat to his harem; and (3) some lived as eunuchs for the sake of the kingdom of heaven. Jesus, John the Baptist and presumably the Apostle Paul fit into this latter category.

Little Children (Matthew 19:13-15)

As evening was approaching, the owners of the household in which Jesus was staying allowed their little children to come to Jesus, perhaps to say "Good night." They were seeking the normal blessing from a rabbi that Jesus would be most inclined to do. Unfortunately, the disciples saw this as an intolerable situation, perhaps out of concern about the extra demand on Jesus or perhaps because this was an interruption to their time with Him. In any case, they rebuked the children and tried to send them away from Jesus. The disciples might well have known that Jesus was quite partial to children had they remembered the lesson given in Matthew 18:1-9. Clearly, little children were greatly attracted to Jesus, as we will see in 21:15.

Mark's Gospel indicates that our Lord was "indignant" at this activity of His disciples. The word Mark used in that verse (Mark 10:14) indicates the depth of His displeasure at seeing His disciples keep the children from Him. Nowhere else is this expression used of Jesus. With a fairly firm rebuke, Jesus commanded the disciples to let the children alone so that they might come to Him. He repeated the statement made earlier that the kingdom of heaven belongs to such as these. Then He fulfilled His ministry to them by laying His hands on them and, as Mark mentions, praying for them.

Besides teaching the importance of children, this passage also illustrates the honesty of the Gospel writers in recording an incident that seems to discredit the disciples. This is especially relevant as we recall that all four Gospels have apostolic credentials, either directly or indirectly.

A Rich Young Man (Matthew 19:16-30)

Although common in John's Gospel, the words "eternal life" do not occur frequently in the synoptic Gospels. In this section we find the words occurring twice. First, in Matthew 19:16 an unidentified person came to Jesus to ask what good thing he might do to obtain eternal life. Later, in verse 29, in a statement reassuring the first disciples about their future, Jesus mentioned that they would inherit eternal life.

The person who came to Jesus to ask what he might do to obtain eternal life has traditionally been called the rich young ruler, based on information given in other Gospels. He is one who "had great wealth" according to verse 22. Furthermore, he is also called young in that same verse. We may assume that his question was genuinely motivated out of concern for his eternal well-being. It is unlikely that this man was a pawn to the nefarious motives of the Pharisees. Nevertheless, the reply of Jesus seems on the surface to be a bit distracting. (We should note that in Matthew's account, the young man asked Jesus, "What good thing must I do?" But in Mark and Luke, the young man asked, "Good teacher, what must I do?" Notice the location of the word "good" in each case, and therefore, the resulting different responses accorded to Jesus.)

After ascribing goodness as a quality belonging only to God (was Jesus implying that the young man had already acknowledged the divinity of Jesus?), Jesus told the young man that if he wished to enter into life, he must keep the commandments. This would not have been a surprising reply because the commandments more than anything else embodied the understanding of the Jewish people about the best way to please God. The young man pressed the point by asking Jesus which particular commandments He meant. This was like the question about which commandment was the greatest. The young man may have been wondering whether there was some new commandment that he would be expected to obey. Jesus replied by listing the last five of the Ten Commandments given in Exodus 20, although in a different order, and a summary command from Leviticus 19:18. These are generally considered to be the commandments focusing on responsibility toward other people. The young man acknowledged that he had kept all of those commandments from his earliest years and wondered what he might still be lacking. We might have expected Jesus to have focused on commandments one through five, which specify our duty toward God. Rather, Jesus turned the young man's thoughts from his inadequate standard of impersonal obedience to the more important issue of excellence of character. Knowing where the young man's heart lay, Jesus said that if he wanted to be complete or perfect he would need to sell his possessions, give his resources to the poor and then follow Him. The young man was being encouraged to invest his resources in treasures in heaven.

We might infer from the story that the wealthy young man hoped to hear that he might gain a favorable destiny by making some charitable contribution to Jesus' cause. "What am I still lacking?" is perhaps a question begging for such a reply. We might have expected Jesus to confront the man about his failure to live completely in obedience to the commandments cited, especially the one from

Leviticus, "Love your neighbor as yourself." Nevertheless, Jesus did not confirm nor contradict the man's assessment of his past life. Rather, even if all had been exactly as the young man mentioned, Jesus indicated there was still something missing—freedom from the bondage of his possessions and "the deceitfulness of wealth" (13:22).

We might also infer that the command of Jesus for the young man to part with his wealth was, in fact, a way of saying that the first four commands, which point to one's responsibility to God and away from idols, were being violated by the man's attachment to his possessions. The young man found this call to be too radical and departed grieved. Mark adds a touching element by saying that despite the young man's unwillingness to follow Jesus, He felt a love for the young man (Mark 10:21).

Alfred Plummer asks the key question about this passage: "How are we to regard this charge to sell everything and give to the poor?"[1] It may have been meant to test this potential disciple's sincerity to follow in the ways of God. Or, it may have been a rule for him and others who want to take the so-called high road of discipleship. Or, it may merely have been a way for Jesus to take the young man down a notch from his lofty perception of himself. Because this particular admonition was given only to this man, it appears Jesus knew that the young man's attachment to wealth and lack of sympathy for the poor would inhibit his discipleship. The virtues he cited were merely sins he had avoided. Jesus was now calling him to a positive virtue, and even more important, a wonderful invitation: "Come, follow me" (Matthew 19:21).

The grief Jesus felt over the loss of this young man led to His comment about the difficulty that rich people have in entering into the kingdom of heaven. Indeed, Jesus said proverbially, "It is easier for a camel to go through the eye of a needle than for a rich man to enter the kingdom of God" (19:24). Some have taken this image to refer to a small gate into the city of Jerusalem that could be entered by a camel only if all cargo was unloaded prior to entry. The image would fit well except that there is no sure evidence that such a gate existed, nor do any ancient expositors adopt this explanation.

Nevertheless, the idea that it would be difficult for rich people to enter the kingdom astonished the disciples perhaps because they still believed, as did many in ancient times, that material prosperity was a sign of the blessing of God. Therefore, if even wealthy people have a difficult time entering the kingdom, they asked, "Who then can be saved?" Rather than answering their question, Jesus said that with God all things are possible, including the entry of the rich man into the kingdom. Perhaps He said this for the sake of the young man who may have been within earshot, to affirm that it is impossible for men to find entry into the kingdom through their own efforts.

Peter, speaking on behalf of the other 11, asked

what their reward would be since they had obeyed the invitation to follow Jesus after abandoning their material possessions. We might have expected Jesus to reprove Peter, advising him of the inappropriateness of such self-concern. But that is not what Jesus did. Rather, He assured them that since they had shared with Him in the hardship of planting the kingdom on earth, they would be leaders of the 12 tribes of Israel in the new society of the kingdom. But not only they; everyone who had made similar sacrifices for the sake of the kingdom, including the sacrifice of houses, family and businesses would receive many times more than what they had abandoned, as well as inherit eternal life. Mark's account (10:29-31) mentions that these rewards, "and with them, persecutions," would be given in this life, and eternal life would be the reward of the next life.

Jesus then uttered the familiar saying, "But many who are first will be last, and many who are last will be first" (Matthew 19:30; 20:16), which serves both as a conclusion to 19:12-29 and an introduction to 20:1-16.

The Vineyard Workers (Matthew 20:1-16)

The parable of the laborers in the vineyard was obviously meant to explain the famous saying, "But many who are first will be last, and many who are last will be first," since those verses sandwich the parable. Again, Matthew presents a parable of the kingdom, saying that the kingdom is like a landowner who at various times during the day hired laborers to help in his vineyard. Laborers went out at the beginning of the day, presumably 6 a.m., three hours later, six hours later, and 11 hours later. Assuming a 12-hour work day, as was common in early times, various laborers would have worked anywhere between 12 hours and one hour.

Apparently the work to be done in the vineyard was of such urgency that throughout the day the landowner continued to look for willing workers. At the 11th hour he found some in the marketplace who had been unemployed all day long. They, too, were sent into the vineyard.

In early times common laborers worked on a per diem basis and received their pay at the end of each day. Since many were poor and lived from hand to mouth, one day's wages would be the next day's meal. Therefore, when pay time came, the landowner instructed his foreman to pay each person one full day's wages beginning with the last group and proceeding to the first group that was hired. All received the same pay, one denarius, which equals one day's wage.

Predictably, when those who were hired earlier saw the generosity of the landowner in giving a full day's wage to those who had worked only one hour, they expected to receive quite a bit more. Their expectation was not rewarded as they received the same amount. The landowner, receiving their complaint, did not deny the truth of their concern but reminded them of the terms of the original agreement he had with them—they would work for him for one day's wage. He also reminded them that as owner of the payroll he could give to each worker as much as he desired. Then in 20:15 he asked the question, "Or are you envious because I am generous?"

Not only was the landowner generous, he was also compassionate, knowing that each person, regardless of the amount of time he worked, would need a full day's wages to provide for his family the next day. The parable is clearly meant to say that in the kingdom of heaven the basis for rewards is not merit but mercy. Those who worked a full day held to the position "it's not fair (to us)." The landowner overruled that idea by saying, "It's more than fair (to all)." He was fair to all, and, to some whose need was just as great as the others, he was merciful.

This parable may have been a mild rebuke to Peter and others who believed that their effort as disciples merited the positions in the kingdom Jesus had earlier assured. Jesus wanted them to understand that others would enter the kingdom and be generously rewarded even if they did not sacrifice as the earliest disciples did. The statement "the first will be last; and the last, first" is illustrated by the last who were hired being paid first and the first who were hired being paid last.

It seems to be an inviolable law of human nature that we vigorously deny mercy and defend justice when we have met its terms, but just as eagerly appeal for mercy over justice when we have not. Likewise, we eagerly deny mercy and defend justice when others have not met the terms of justice.

Prediction of Death (Matthew 20:17-19)

The final march to Jerusalem was now about to begin. These verses are commonly called the third announcement of the suffering and death of Jesus, although this is the fourth recorded announcement in Matthew (17:12 was a statement given only to the three who accompanied Him at the transfiguration). Mark indicated that this announcement astonished and frightened the Twelve. No doubt this was a recollection of Peter's personal experience.

Verse 17 implies that Jesus invited only the 12 disciples to accompany Him to Jerusalem, leaving others behind. During their journey Jesus gave the prediction, and specifically identified that Jerusalem would be the scene of His suffering, and that the method of His death would be crucifixion at the hands of Gentiles. The alliance between the chief priests, scribes and the Gentile leaders might seem strange to the disciples, except for the reference to the crucifixion that could be carried out only with Gentiles' cooperation. At the end of the prediction, Jesus again assured the disciples that He would be raised on the third day. The text gives no indication of the response by the disciples.

Request for Privilege (Matthew 20:20-28)

Undoubtedly, as they began to understand that

the end was at hand and that the kingdom was about to be inaugurated, the disciples began nervously to consider their part in the kingdom. Although all 12 had been assured earlier (19:28) that they would have a preferential place in the kingdom, the sons of Zebedee, James and John, thought that perhaps they should have an even more prestigious place. Matthew indicates that their mother came to Jesus with the peculiar request for such preference, whereas Mark and Luke say James and John took the initiative to ask. Because Matthew seems eager at times to protect the reputation of the disciples, we might tend to think he was using the mother here for that purpose. Such may not be the case because the mother of James and John was Salome, the sister of the mother of Jesus (see Matthew 27:56; Mark 15:40; and John 19:25).[2] This special relationship might make it reasonable to assume there would be such preferential treatment given in the kingdom, and it is not unlikely that an aunt would take such initiative on behalf of her sons. Obviously, however, it was not merely a concern of Salome but also of her sons.

Matthew's use of "one . . . at your right and the other at your left" (Matthew 20:21) may well be intended to correspond with similar terminology in 27:38, where two others are on the right and left of Jesus, participating in a similar "cup" of suffering.

The reference in verses 22 and 23 to drinking the cup recalls the language of Isaiah 51:17, 22, as

well as Jeremiah 49:12. The self-confident reply of
James and John clearly indicated that they did not
understand the nature of the fury of that cup.
Nevertheless, as with the rich young ruler, whose
self-confidence Jesus did not contradict, we find
Jesus again refraining from such argumentation.
Rather, He affirmed that they would drink from
that cup, but granting preferential positions in the
kingdom was the prerogative of His Father.

The other 10 disciples were aware of this discussion and became indignant at the sons of thunder. Jesus used the opportunity to teach them all
about leadership in the kingdom by contrasting
the way Gentile leaders use their authority to the
approach He had taken as a servant-leader. Servanthood in the kingdom is the root to greatness,
whereas extreme greatness is entered through extreme servanthood (20:26-27).

Verse 28 is very important because it includes a
rare but very important word translated "ransom." The doctrine surrounding this word has
many interpretations because the word suggests a
payment being made by someone to someone else.
Obviously, the payment is the life of Jesus, but
who is making that payment to whom remains an
interesting question. Jesus as the Son of Man did
not come to earth merely to be great or even to be
first, but rather to give His life as a ransom, an
even more extreme idea. Plummer humbly notes,
"the way in which this ransom sets men free is beyond our comprehension."[3] This verse indicates
how clearly Jesus understood His mission. His

preexistence is implied by the word "come." In all
cases except one in the New Testament Jesus used
the concept of coming to the world rather than being born. (Even when He indicated His birth in
John 18:37, He added the modifying phrase "for
this I came into the world.")

No greater impetus for a proper use of authority could be given to the disciples than the example of Jesus Himself. He indicated that the
sacrificing of His life to set others free came at His
own initiative ("give his life as a ransom for
many," Matthew 20:28). The use of the word
"many" is used by some to substantiate a doctrine
of limited atonement; the indefinite "many" does
not mean that He did not intend to redeem some,
or that He did not die for some. Rather, it is in opposition to the idea of one, implying that He was
not sacrificing Himself for personal advantage;
one life would be sacrificed for the ultimate advantage of many who would take advantage of the
gift of redemption. (First Timothy 2:6 and 1 John
2:2 indicate the intended universality of the sacrifice.) This section that began with a request for
self-aggrandizement properly ends with an affirmation of self-sacrifice.

The Healing of the Blind (Matthew 20:29-34)

The route of Jesus to Jerusalem went through
Jericho, a city northwest of the Dead Sea, lying in
the lowland of the Jordan River. The ascent from
Jericho to Jerusalem was steep, but nonetheless
traversed by a great multitude who followed Jesus.

Enroute they passed two blind men who, upon hearing that Jesus was one of the travelers, repeatedly yelled, "Lord, Son of David, have mercy on us!" The multitude was eager to silence these men because the "Son of David" term was clearly messianic. At this point, either because of their concern for Jesus as He approached a city that would not welcome such messianic aspirations, or out of overinflated piety reflected in jealously guarding the title of Messiah, the people were clearly not moved with compassion.

Jesus stopped the entourage and addressed the two blind men, asking what they wanted Him to do. Their reply was simple and obvious. They wanted to receive their sight. Matthew indicates that Jesus performed the miracle of restoring sight by touching their eyes. The two then became part of the group traveling to Jerusalem.

Mark and Luke also report this event, but Mark particularly provides additional detail. One of the two is identified as Bartimaeus. He is described as a blind beggar who was sitting by the road. Mark also indicates that Jesus called for the man to be brought to Him. Mark also provides other details that certainly indicate a first-hand witness to the incident (Mark 10:46-52). If the crowd had any doubt that "Son of David" should be applied to Jesus, perhaps this incident convinced them otherwise. For surely, many of them, including Bartimaeus, were among those who took up the chant in Matthew 21:9, "Hosanna to the Son of David!"

"Hosanna" (Matthew 21:1-11)

Although chapters 21 and 22 are part of the fifth narrative of Matthew's Gospel, chapter 21 clearly begins a new major section of the Gospel. The triumphal entry of Jesus into Jerusalem begins the final act of His life on earth. East of Jerusalem, on the other side of the Kidron Valley, was the Mount of Olives from which Jesus dispatched two disciples into a nearby village to procure a donkey and colt for His entry into Jerusalem. Either by a prearranged signal or supernatural means (the text does not indicate the means by which Jesus was assured that His words would be followed), the two disciples would find the beasts and gain permission for their use by saying, "The Lord needs them." Presumably the owner knew who the Lord was and may have even been a fellow disciple.

Matthew indicates that this activity was a direct fulfillment of the prophecy given in Zechariah 9:9, where it is proclaimed that the daughter of Zion, the daughter of Jerusalem, should rejoice because her king would be coming to her mounted humbly on a colt. This method of entering Jerusalem was anything but the coronation of a king, as might be expected after a successful campaign. Rather it was a king coming to His people with a message of peace. The gentleness of the demeanor of the king and of the beast upon which He rode was understood to be a peaceful sign and one very much welcomed.

The disciples found the arrangements exactly as

Jesus had foretold and were able to follow His directions precisely. As they began spreading their garments on the animal to serve as a quasi-saddle for Jesus, others recognized the special occasion and began laying their garments on the pathway of Jesus to provide a red-carpet welcome. Others cut branches from nearby palm trees to add to the carpet effect.

Celebration and excitement were in the air as the multitude who paraded before Jesus were crying, "Hosanna to the Son of David! Blessed is he who comes in the name of the Lord! Hosanna in the highest!" These words clearly express messianic longing. The word "hosanna" literally means "save us." Rather than a plea of desperation, they were clearly an ejaculation of exultation and expectation. They did not understand the nature of the messianic work that Jesus would perform, but they clearly understood Him to be a very special person upon whom the mantle of Messiah must have fallen. Nevertheless, their understanding was not complete because they were explaining to others who might not have known Jesus that He was a prophet from Nazareth in Galilee (Matthew 21:11).

The event certainly moved the city. Jerusalem was "stirred" by the entrance of Jesus in this uncharacteristically self-magnifying act. Creating such a public stir may indeed have been His very purpose for staging this episode. J.C. Ryle notes, "The whole transaction is singularly at variance with the past tenor of our Lord's life. It is curiously unlike the ways of Him who did not 'cry, nor strive, nor let His voice be heard in the streets,'—who withdrew Himself from the multitude on other occasions,—and said to those He healed, 'See thou say nothing to any man' (Mark 1:44)."[4]

If Jesus, indeed, wanted to make a public sensation, this was clearly the time to do it, for it was Passover when the whole surrounding neighborhood of a 20-mile radius would be crowding the city. Likewise, many pilgrims from far away would be coming to this annual rite of remembrance of the Exodus, which included the slaughter of the Passover lamb and the observance of the *seder*. Barclay notes that 30 years later than this, the Romans took a census of the lambs slain in Jerusalem during Passover. Nearly 250,000 lambs were slaughtered. Passover regulations insisted that a minimum of 10 people participate in each *seder*. If these figures were accurate, more than two and one-half million people crowded into Jerusalem during this time.

Barclay is likewise fascinated by the intention of Jesus in this somewhat uncharacteristic act. He offers two suggestions, the first of which seems more likely. Jewish prophets of old often used dramatic acts to make symbolic statements of a message that was extremely important, and likely not communicated as well by mere words. Ahijah's garment torn into 12 pieces for Jeroboam (1 Kings 11:29-32) and Jeremiah's yoke (Jeremiah 27:1-6) are two examples given by Barclay. Similarly, Jesus' dramatic and literal fulfillment of Zechariah 9:9 would be viewed as a deliberate messianic claim.

The other possibility is that this spectacular entry was a prelude to the cleansing of the temple. In 175 B.C. the Syrian despot Antiochus Ephiphanes came into Jerusalem intending to stamp out Judaism and replace it with Hellenistic culture. Parading into the temple, he defiled it by sacrificing swines' flesh on the altar to Zeus, the Olympian god. He also turned the temple chambers into public brothels. The Maccabee brothers rose up against him and eventually delivered Jerusalem from such sacrilege. Second Maccabees 10:7 indicates that Judas Maccabees then entered Jerusalem to a similar kind of fanfare with tree branches strewn before him amid much celebration and the singing of psalms. No doubt, many saw Judas Maccabees in a messianic role. Coming to the temple in a dramatic fashion was clearly anticipated by Malachi 3:1. And Jesus was now set to do just that.

The Temple Cleansing (Matthew 21:12-17)

If the pompous entrance of Jesus into Jerusalem seemed to be uncharacteristic of Him, even more so the next event. For He entered the temple and began overturning the tables and booths of the money changers and those who were selling the doves. He chased out of the temple the people who were involved in the merchandising, citing several Old Testament passages angrily, " 'My house will be called a house of prayer,' but you are making it a den of robbers" (Matthew 21:13).

The synoptic Gospel writers are uniform in placing this event after the triumphal entry. John's Gospel indicates that there was an earlier cleansing (John 2:13-17). We should not be surprised that this would be the response of Jesus anytime He found the temple to be so misused. The reason for the ire of Jesus is documented eloquently by William Barclay. In the temple precincts were the bazaars of Annas, who had been high priest and whose son Caiaphas was now the high priest. Annas had a tidy business going in the temple because it was incumbent on all Jewish worshipers to present unblemished sacrifices during Passover. In many cases pilgrims would come to Jerusalem from afar and bring their own sacrifices, which almost without exception would be rejected because a blemish would be found. They could then buy a dove or a lamb in the temple, but at a highly inflated price—perhaps as much as 10 times over the going rate outside of the temple. The exploitation of poor and simple worshipers for the profit of a high priestly family must have angered Jesus. The stated reason for His anger was His zeal that the temple remain a house of prayer. No reaction to His temple cleansing is stated by Matthew, but we might well assume that the episode contributed greatly to the anger of the family of Annas later when Jesus stood before them on trial.

While Jesus was in the temple, people seeking healing came to Him and were successfully ministered to by Jesus. Chief priests and scribes who saw these miracles and heard children who were crying out, "Hosanna to the Son of David," became enraged. They suggested to Jesus that it was His responsibility to quiet the children because, in their view, the messianic appellations of the children were blasphemous. As He often did, Jesus replied by using Scripture. He asked the Jewish leaders whether they had ever read Psalm 8:2, "From the lips of children and infants you have ordained praise." Having cleansed the temple, ministered to those who were needy and silenced His most recent critics, Jesus left both the temple and Jerusalem to depart for the nearby town of Bethany where He lodged, presumably in the home of Lazarus, Mary and Martha.

The Fig Tree (Matthew 21:18-22)

The next day as Jesus and the disciples made their way back to Jerusalem, they passed a lone fig tree by the road. The tree was obviously out of sync with nature, because it should not have had leaves during the month of April. The presence of leaves would also have indicated that the first of two crops of figs had already come. Normally, the first crop would come in the month of June and the leaves would grow thereafter. Mark's account of this incident demonstrates his knowledge of the seasonal nature of fig trees by mentioning, "It was not the season for the figs" (Mark 11:13).

Because the tree demonstrated something it had not actually performed, Jesus cursed the tree by announcing that it should never be fruitful again. William Barclay states that because the tree was so out of line with its natural and seasonal cycle, Jesus could readily determine that the tree was already diseased. In this case His prophetic curse was really more a statement of fact than a statement of cause.

Nevertheless, like the two preceding episodes (the triumphal entry and the temple cleansing), this event also seems to be a bit out of character for Jesus. Why would He (a) look for figs on a tree out of season and (b) curse that tree for not bearing that which was not even expected? Most commentators see this event to be prophetic in nature. A meaning far greater than the immediate cursing of the tree was intended.

The fig tree was often used as a symbol of Palestine because of its fruitfulness. Like all other countries, Judah went through historical cycles, and this was so especially with its religion. In the Old Testament the people of God were sometimes found to be full of faith and religious vitality, and other times full of faithlessness, which led them into exile. This particular moment in Judah's history was one of religious fervor, but the piety was more external and superficial than internal and genuine. The fig tree symbolized Israel's season of fruitfulness but without the expected fruit.

Seeing the tree wither so rapidly caused the disciples to marvel and ask how it happened. They did not ask Jesus why He cursed it because they also understood the cycles of nature and recognized it to be a diseased tree. The reply of Jesus centered on the importance of praying with faith. The saying Jesus used about the potency of prayer, namely, a mountain being moved and cast into the sea, was a common metaphor for something that would be impossible to accomplish. It taught the disciples that they should not put limitations upon the ability of God to achieve the impossible. We should not assume that Jesus was sanctioning the use of prayer for destructive purposes. His intentions are always redemptive, and even in the cursing of the fig tree, the positive lesson it demonstrated to the disciples was worth the result upon an already diseased tree.

Authority Challenged (Matthew 21:23-27)

Jesus again entered the temple and began a more peaceful teaching ministry, although perhaps we ought not to think that cleansing the temple was a one-time event. Both Mark and Luke say that Jesus began to cast out the buyers and sellers. He may have interfered with the temple trafficking in less conspicuous ways on other occasions. Perhaps it was such interference or the teaching of Jesus that led the chief priests and elders to ask, "By what authority are you doing these things? And who gave you this authority?" (Matthew 21:23).

The Jewish leaders may have been concerned about the near riotous situation that occurred the day before, beginning with the triumphal entry and culminating in the scene at the temple. They were eager to placate Roman leadership, especially during a time when the population of the city was so swollen. No doubt an even stronger motivation for their questioning was their effort to get Him to say something that they could use against Him. The reply of Jesus, far from being evasive, was a question that would lead to an answer to their own question. By asking whether they accepted the authority of John the Baptist, Jesus gave them an opportunity to declare whether they believed John's message. If they believed John's message, then it was clear that Jesus clearly was the Messiah whom John had introduced. That messianic position was certainly the credential for the authority He was exercising.

The elders and chief priests quickly recognized their dilemma. They did not believe John to be a legitimate prophet because they disregarded his message. They were not willing, however, to confess that publicly because it was clear that the masses of people in Judah did believe in John. Their weak and evasive reply received an answer of noncommittal by Jesus as well. If they were unwilling to take an unpopular stand, He would not give them the satisfaction of an answer either.

Nevertheless, Plummer indicates that the Jewish leaders gained a slight advantage from this exchange, because Jesus refused to disclaim the authority that others ascribed to Him.[5] On this claim of messianic fulfillment, the Jewish leaders would begin to build their case.

The Two Sons (Matthew 21:28-32)

As is often the case, Matthew then presented a triplet of parables. All three parables were illustrations of the moral lesson He had demonstrated by the withering fig tree, namely, that the empty profession of religious piety by the leaders in Jerusalem merited severe judgment. In the first parable Jesus asked the members of the Sanhedrin to consider a contrast of sons. One son was quick to obey his father's command to work in the vineyard, but then failed to do so. The other son verbally refused the assignment but then afterward went out and obeyed. Jesus asked, "Which of the two did what his father?" The Jews rightly responded that the second son was the obedient one.

The meaning of the parable is patently obvious, but Jesus wanted to press the point home. The first son represents the religious establishment of Jerusalem, which on the surface seems to want to please God, but in reality chooses to indulge itself. The second son, Jesus said, represents tax collectors and prostitutes, "who are entering the kingdom of God ahead of you" (Matthew 21:31). These are people who profess no piety but find a time and place for repentance that would qualify them for entrance into the kingdom.

Neither son was perfect, and neither were the religious leaders or the tax collectors and prostitutes exemplary individuals. An ideal son would both promise obedience and perform it. But for the purpose of the parable, two categories of indi-

viduals are contrasted so that Jesus might declare
to the Jewish leaders that their role and value in
the kingdom might be quite different than what
they and others would expect. Jesus applied the
lesson and declared His belief in John the Baptist
by saying that he came to the Jewish nation as a
righteous individual whom the Jewish leaders did
not believe but whom the tax collectors and prostitutes did accept. Jesus pressed the point even
further by saying that after the Jewish leaders saw
the massive movement of repentance by even the
most unworthy of Israelites, the religious leaders
were not moved in the slightest toward God.

The Wicked Tenants (Matthew 21:33-46)

The second parable communicates virtually the
same message. The parable of the two sons refers
to the past while the parable of the wicked tenants
deals with the present and the future. It was a
very strong warning to the Jewish leaders that Jesus knew their intentions to kill Him and that in
doing so they would invoke the wrath of God
upon themselves. The imagery of Israel as a vineyard is used by the prophets to great advantage
and with differing purposes (see Isaiah 5:1-7; Jeremiah 2:21; Ezekiel 15:1-6; 19:10-14; Hosea 10:1).

In this parable Jesus gave the Jewish leaders the
answer to their question about the source of His
authority. The slaves and the son went to the tenants on the authority of the landowner, whom the
listeners would readily understand to be God.
The slaves who were sent to receive the produce

but were rejected were understood to be the prophets sent by God but rejected by Israel.

After violently rejecting the slaves, the tenants, who represented the Jewish leaders who were responsible to produce fruit in the land, were confronted by the landowner's son. He was sent on the same mission but with the expectation that he would be respected. Rather than recognizing the authority of the son, the tenants took the opportunity to kill the heir of the estate and steal his inheritance. The reference to throwing him out of the vineyard and killing him was obviously used by Jesus to predict His execution outside the city of Jerusalem. Jesus did not leave any doubt that the tenants knew the identity of the son. They fully recognized that he was, in fact, the heir. And so Jesus implied that the Jewish antagonists also understood His sacred identity.

Jesus then asked what seems in Luke and Mark to be a rhetorical question, "What would the landowner do to the unfaithful tenants?" In Matthew's account the rhetorical question was answered, not by Jesus, but by the listeners who indicated rightly that the landowner would bring the "wretches" to an end and rent out the vineyard to others who would respect him and yield to him the fruit of the vineyard.

Jesus seized this moment of illumination to point out the danger in which these Jewish leaders should now see themselves. Clearly they were aware of Psalm 118, which tells about the builders rejecting a stone that later became the chief cor-

nerstone. The landowner's son was rejected, and
the cornerstone was rejected. Nevertheless, God's
purposes would not be thwarted.

The application of these parables was made by
Jesus. The kingdom of God was to be taken away
from the Jewish leaders and be given to "a people
who will produce its fruit." The interpretation of
the parable of the wicked tenants could not be
made clearer. The Jewish leaders and nation
would be judged by God for their rejection of His
prophets and Son. The benefits of the kingdom
would be given to someone else. Furthermore,
"He who falls on this stone will be broken to
pieces, but he on whom it falls will be crushed"
(Matthew 21:44). The interpretation of the imagery of the stone also was made clear. Not only
would those who rejected the cornerstone be humiliated, but they would also be destroyed by that
very stone.

So plain and clear were the implications of these
teachings that the chief priests and Pharisees understood that Jesus was speaking about them.
Consequently, they desired to seize Him immediately, but they feared the multitudes who considered Jesus to be a prophet. At this point they
refrained from taking vindictive action.

The Wedding Banquet (Matthew 22:1-14)

Jesus continued to speak to the Jewish leaders in
parables (22:1; the plural may indicate that two
parables are found in verses 2-14). This third parable in the triad also suggests that God finds the

Jewish nation, and particularly the leaders, deficient in their response to Him. The circumstances of the marriage feast in the parable are quite normal for first-century Semitic culture. A lavish feast would be announced, invitations would be sent out without a precise day or time mentioned and when the feast had been prepared, servants would be sent to instruct the invitees to come promptly. In Semitic cultures it was extremely insulting to accept an invitation initially and then refuse to honor it. The parable shows that some who were invited simply paid no attention to the summons and went about their own business (v. 5). Others added injury to insult by seizing the servants, abusing them and killing them. The enraged king sent his armies to the city where these murderers lived and destroyed both the murderers and their city.

Some commentators see verses 6 and 7 as additions supplied by the Evangelist after the sacking of Jerusalem by the Romans. In truth, the parable does read well, going from verse 5 to 8. There is no textual evidence, however, to exclude verses 6 and 7 from the original parable. The message of the parable is stated in verses 8 and 9 in which the king tells the servants that the ones who were originally invited were not worthy to come to the wedding, but that others who had not been invited would now be included. Verse 10 adds that the latter group eventually were brought to the wedding hall so that it was filled with dinner guests.

This parable has great affinity with the one found in Luke 14:16-24. There are striking differences in detail and language, but the lesson is essentially the same. We might assume that Jesus gave many parables that were similar to one another, adapting them at different times to the audience and situation of the moment.

Matthew 22:11-14 seems to be a second parable, or at least a second lesson added to the first parable. Jewish folklore had a number of stories about kings and garments. Jesus might well have known some of these stories and adapted one of them for this moment. He wanted to emphasize that even though people not originally invited to the feast would now be invited (presumably Gentiles), there would still be a royal protocol for them to observe. The man who was not dressed properly for the wedding clearly represents someone who refused the king's provisions for attendance. Most likely this story is related to one that shows that the king himself would supply the garments for the wedding feast, since the common man and certainly the poorer class would have no means for dressing themselves properly. In this case the guest without proper wedding clothes simply ignored royal protocol and chose to come in his dirty inferior clothes. The king was quite justified in banishing the guest from the feast. Verse 13 is an allusion to previous references Jesus made about Gehenna, which would be the ultimate fate of those not included in the kingdom.

Verse 14, "For many are invited, but few are

chosen," fits in very well with the first part of this parable ending at verse 10, and may more reasonably be applied to verses 2-10. Whether or not the verse is meant to apply to the first part of the parable, the second part of the parable   or both parts, it is clear that Jesus put the final results back in the hands of the king who gave the wedding feast. That is to say that   while the king extended a universal invitation, he also retained authority over who would actually be allowed entrance to the kingdom. Certainly the latter part of the parable (verses 11-14) indicates that this is a reasonable interpretation of verse 14.

Taxes to Caesar (Matthew 22:15-22)

The three parables made an impact on the Pharisees. They were determined to find a way to get Jesus to condemn Himself through His words. Knowing that Jesus was a man of principle and not expedience, they believed that if they could pose a question or an issue in such a way as to force Him to declare a truth that would be self-condemning, they would then be able to accomplish their goal of having Him arrested and destroyed.

Since their previous attempts had been futile when they confronted Jesus directly, they now sent their followers along with Herodians to pose a deadly question to Jesus. The fact that disciples of the Pharisees were sent with Herodians indicates that both groups, which would normally be opponents, were in agreement about the need to

silence Jesus. Herodians were a political party
who supported the Roman government, whereas
the Pharisees were separatists and opposed the
government, as we have already seen.

Apart from its malicious intent, the question
about tribute was not an unreasonable one to ask
a rabbi. Of course, Jesus saw through their deception and their flattery (v. 16), and asked that
a coin be brought to Him. The denarius that was
handed to Him would have had on one side an
image of Caesar, the Roman emperor. The coin
represented many benefits enjoyed by all in the
Roman Empire (including the Jews): security,
organization, facilities, government and economy. Perhaps that is why Jesus turned the issue
slightly in His answer. The question had asked
whether it was right to *give* the poll tax to Caesar. Jesus used a different word and said that it
was proper to *pay* or *render* to Caesar that which
he rightfully deserved. The tribute to Rome was
not a gift but a payment of a debt. And by making such a payment, no citizen, regardless of
how religious he might be, would be guilty of
co-opting his obligation to God. However, Jesus
was not content merely to say that it was fitting
and proper to pay for services rendered. He
went beyond that to claim that all people should
render to God the things that are God's. Clearly
it would be understood that the greater responsi-
bilities of all people lie in the spiritual realm,
since the authority of God is much broader than
the authority even of Rome. The questioners

knew they had met their match and left marveling at the wisdom of Jesus.

Marriage in the Resurrection (Matthew 22:23-33)

The next volley of questions came from Sadducees on that same day. Although the Sadducees were not many in number, they were the wealthy, aristocratic, governing class. Chief priests were Sadducees. They differed from the Pharisees both politically and religiously. Politically they were quite ready to accept the government of the Romans or any group that would assure them the maintenance of their privileged position. Religiously they accepted only the five books of Moses as Scripture. Since they believed that those books did not warrant a belief in resurrection, they refused the doctrine of immortality.

Pharisees had made various attempts in the past to demonstrate from the Pentateuch the legitimacy of their belief in resurrection. Very strange portions of Scripture were used, such as "This people will rise up," which might seem to be a reasonable evidence of resurrection except for the fact that the verse adds, "and go a whoring after the gods of the strangers of the land" (Deuteronomy 31:16, KJV). Fanciful interpretations of many Scriptures were created by the Pharisees from the books of Moses to argue for resurrection.

Knowing that Jesus accepted the legitimacy of the prophets and writings, the Sadducees knew that He probably agreed with the Pharisees about resurrection. Therefore, they posed to Him a most unlikely case that encompassed the Jewish custom called levirate marriage. Drawn from Deuteronomy 25:5-10, this principle requires that when a man's brother dies, and the deceased brother's wife is childless, the surviving brother must take the wife of his deceased brother and help her conceive a son so that the name of her husband will continue. In the story posed by the Sadducees, a woman became a wife successively of seven brothers who all died without leaving her offspring. Finally, she died. The question posed by the Sadducees was, "Whose wife would she be in the resurrection?"

Jesus replied by telling them that on two accounts they were ignorant of the Scriptures and of the power of God. First, they supposed that life in the resurrection was exactly as life on earth. He instructed them that relationships are significantly different in the resurrection because people do not marry or have marriage partners in that realm.

Jesus then astonished all His listeners by doing what the Pharisees up until now had failed to do, namely, using a verse from the Pentateuch to prove conclusively the reality of the resurrection. He cited a commonly used statement in which God calls Himself the God of Abraham after Abraham had already died (for example, Genesis 26:24; 28:13). In Exodus 3:6, 15:16 and 4:5, God also calls Himself the God of Abraham, Isaac and Jacob after all three had died. The obvious inference is that those who had died in this world are still alive to God, for He cannot be a God to those who have no existence. The strength of the argumentation was even stronger by the fact that in Matthew 22:31 Jesus asked, "Have you not read what God said to you . . . ?" The Sadducees had these very familiar verses right in front of their eyes all these generations and had never yet seen the force of them. That is why the multitudes who heard this brilliant answer by Jesus were astonished (22:33).

The Greatest Command (Matthew 22:34-40)

The Pharisees were undoubtedly most pleased about this convincing reply by Jesus but still not willing to accept the messiahship of Jesus. Therefore, gathering themselves again (22:34), they put forward a legal expert who asked Jesus a common question, "Which is the great commandment in the Law?" Throughout Jewish history many rabbis and scribes had debated this question. Would it be possible to sum up the hundreds of laws into one pithy principle? Most had come to the conclusion that it was not possible, and the Pharisees in particular insisted, therefore, that all of the details of every major and minor law be scrupulously followed.

Unlike the Pharisees, Jesus did offer one principle upon which all the others were based and the fulfillment of which would entail obedience to all, namely, "Love the Lord your God with all your heart and with all your soul and with all your mind" (22:37). Jesus called this verse, drawn from

Deuteronomy 6:5, the great and foremost commandment. But quickly He declared that a second and similar principle was nearly as important, namely, loving one's neighbor as one's self, taken from Leviticus 19:18.

These two commandments are seen to be of such magnitude, because not only do they prescribe the objects for human love but also the intensity. God is to be loved with the entire being of a person: heart, soul, and mind. The neighbor is to be loved as much as one loves himself. Because the objects of love and the intensity of love are so universal and powerful, Jesus is able to say that all of the law and the prophets depend on these two commandments. They fulfill the elementary precepts of the Pentateuch and also the more advanced teaching given by the prophets.

The Main Question (Matthew 22:41-45)

Having successfully outmaneuvered the trick questions of the Pharisees, Herodians, Sadducees and a legal expert, Jesus took the initiative and asked them a question: "What do you think about the Christ? Whose son is he?" Knowing in advance that their answer would be "the Son of David," Jesus was ready to put them on the horns of a dilemma. He asked them how David, under divine inspiration, could call the Messiah "LORD." Jesus quoted Psalm 110:1 which says, "The Lord says to my Lord: 'Sit at my right hand . . .'." The first reference to the Lord is to God, and the second is to the Messiah. Jesus then asked the Pharisees that if David called the Messiah "Lord," how could the Messiah merely be a physical descendant of David?

What was the purpose of Jesus in this? As we have seen earlier, Jesus was reluctant to release to the masses His identity as the Messiah. This was because of the false understanding that many had about the nature of the Messiah as merely a physical descendant from David who would be a great political and military conqueror. Jesus used this verse from Psalm 110 to show the Pharisees and others that David did not consider the Messiah to be merely a physical descendant but to be someone to whom he owed obeisance and worship.

The implication of this is that the Messiah is not only the Son of David but the Son of God. Jesus left the question lingering, "If then David calls him 'Lord,' how can he be his son?" The intention of Jesus here was to cause His hearers to begin thinking of messiahship in terms other than political and military. Rather, if indeed He was the Son of God, His mission might include the more divine attributes and functions that the Jews commonly associated with the Divine Being.

By this time all of Jesus' opponents had been successfully engaged and defeated. None entertained the delusion any longer that they would be able to outmaneuver Jesus intellectually or doctrinally. Therefore, as Matthew reports, "from that day on no one dared to ask him any more questions" (Matthew 22:46).

We have seen in this fifth narrative three domi-

nant themes. Throughout the four chapters the
disciples were either in the background or the
foreground receiving much needed instruction
and training. The primary content of the teaching,
both in His parables and responses to the tests of
His opponents, focused on kingdom citizenship
and who qualified for it. In addition, the storm
clouds of conflict began gathering over the life of
Jesus as His opponents became increasingly
threatened by His popularity, His power and, particularly, His messianic claims.

Endnotes

1. Alfred Plummer, *An Exegetical Commentary on
   The Gospel According to St. Matthew* (Grand Rapids: Baker Book House, 1982), p. 267.
2. Ibid., p. 277.
3. Ibid., p. 280.
4. J.C. Ryle's *Expository Thoughts on the Gospels*,
   (Grand Rapids, MI: Zondervan Publishing
   House), reprint 1951, p. 263.
5. Plummer, p. 294.

CHAPTER 10

The Coming Kingdom

Matthew 23-25

The fifth and final discourse of Jesus was delivered to multitudes and to His disciples. The discourse seems to be a continuation of the ministry of Jesus in the temple. In the previous few chapters the enemies of Jesus posed several problems that they had hoped would trick Jesus into impaling Himself on His own words. Matthew 22:46 makes it clear that they knew they had met their match and they would need to take another approach to finding a charge against Jesus that would result in His condemnation.

The fifth discourse was delivered in two different locations and concerned two different topics. The monologue in chapter 23 exposes the spiritual corruption of the Pharisees and occurred while Jesus and the disciples were still in the temple. Chapters 24 and 25 comprise the apocalyptic discourse of Jesus and began as Jesus and the disciples were leaving the temple, traveling through

the Kidron Valley, and continued as they reached
the Mount of Olives where Jesus gave an extended
teaching.

The Haughtiness of the Pharisees (Matthew 23:1-12)

The strong denouncement of the Pharisees in
chapter 23 may seem to be uncharacteristic of Jesus' temperament. He was the One, after all, who
taught that people should not condemn or judge
others (7:1-6). Why did He so sternly condemn
the Pharisees? The answer seems to be in verse 2
where He stated that the scribes and Pharisees
have seated themselves in the chair of Moses. In
other words, Jesus was not denouncing them
merely as humans who had fallen victim to the
usual array of sins and faults of humanity, but as
spiritual leaders who purported to be the van-
guards of Mosaic truth. As Jesus stated in Matthew 5:17-19, He did not wish to abolish the law;
in fact, He came to fill the law full of new meaning and taught His followers not to undermine the
importance of the law in any way. Presumably,
those who set themselves up as the strongest advocates of the law of Moses had the greater responsibility for living according to its precepts. This is
where Jesus faulted the Pharisees.

To His followers Jesus said that they should listen and comply with the teachings of the Pharisees but not use the Pharisees as their examples
for life. The Pharisees were hypocritical by prescribing teachings that they themselves did not

follow in their own lives. It must be understood
that when Jesus said, "Do everything they tell
you," He was referring to the teaching of the
scribes and Pharisees that was truly Mosaic, for
verses 4 and following indicate that the scribes
and Pharisees enjoyed prescribing many other religious duties ("heavy loads") for other people.
These heavy loads were certainly not part of the
expectation of Moses nor of God. In their zeal to
give prescriptions for every possible circumstance
in life, the scribes and Pharisees wrote 50 huge
volumes of rules and regulations. Contrast this
with the simple formulas Jesus cited at the end of
chapter 22—two simple principles that summed
up the law and the prophets. The Pharisees preferred to heap law upon law and then pile these
expectations on the shoulders of other people,
making religious life a staggering impossibility.
And then to add insult to injury, the Pharisees
were not in the least bit interested in helping people with the weight of the religious burdens they
had put upon them.

It must not be concluded, however, that the
Pharisees were uncaring about the opinions of
their fellow man. Far from it. As verse 5 asserts,
they performed their religious life publicly for the
very purpose of being noticed by other people.
Specifically, they arranged their wardrobe so that
others would notice them. They wore phylacteries, which were small scrolls of a portion of the
law inside little pouches that were strapped to the
forehead and to the wrist as demonstrations of

their obedience to Exodus 13:9, which indicates
that "this observance will be for you like a sign on
your hand and a reminder on your forehead." The
remainder of the verse indicates that "the law of
the LORD is to be on your lips," but presumably
the Pharisees stopped short of putting a phylac-
tery inside their mouth. They did make sure,
however, that their phylacteries were quite large
so that everyone would notice them.

Furthermore, they embellished their clothing
by putting very long tassels on their garments.
Numbers 15:37-41 and Deuteronomy 22:12 indicate that God wanted His people to have fringes
on the borders of their garments as remembrances
of the commandments of God. The Pharisees
must have thought that the longer the tassels
were, the more they would be noticed and the
more their own piety would be admired.

Besides customizing their wardrobe, the scribes
and Pharisees also positioned themselves for special honor. At banquets they would seek the seats
closest to the host to demonstrate that they were
people of privilege, and in the synagogue they
sought to sit where the elders would be positioned, facing the congregation so others could see
them. In the marketplace the scribes and Pharisees
enjoyed being greeted with terms of great respect,
such as "Rabbi."

Jesus then warned His listeners that, unlike the
scribes and Pharisees, they should specifically not
allow themselves to be called by honorary titles.
They should not be called "Rabbi" because in

matters of religion there really is only one Teacher. All others are brothers, and to insist that other brothers use titles of respect and honor not only divides the brotherhood unnecessarily but also diminishes the role of the one true Teacher. The word used here is not the usual word for "teacher" and occurs only in this location in the New Testament. It refers to someone who guides other people by going before them in a position of leadership.

Furthermore, Jesus insisted that His listeners not allow other people to call them "father," because there is only one true Father, the one who is in heaven. The title "Father" was used as an extremely respectful reference for the spiritual elders of Israel. The listeners of Jesus were admonished not to use this title for anyone on earth.

The intent for these prohibitions is given in verses 11 and 12. True piety does not seek to be noticed but seeks a lowly place of unseen service. The scribes and Pharisees were at fault by seeking to exalt themselves and thereby violated the essence of the very virtue they wished to be known for, namely, their religious and pietistic fervor.

Seven Woes (Matthew 23:13-36)

Having denounced the scribes and Pharisees for their haughtiness, Jesus then put the spotlight on their hypocrisy. Seven or eight woes are poured out upon the Pharisees because of their hypocrisy. Most likely there are seven woes because verse 14

is not found in the earliest and best Greek manuscripts. The woes are found in verses 13, 15, 16,
23, 25, 27 and 29. In each case, except for the one
beginning in verse 16, Jesus began by saying,
"Woe to you, teachers of the law and Pharisees,
you hypocrites!" These verses are described aptly
by Plummer as "thunder in their unanswerable severity, and like lightning in their unsparing expo-
sure. . . . they illuminate while they strike."[1]

We have already seen the word "woe" used
against Korazin and Bethsaida (11:21) and against
the world (18:7). "Woe" may also be translated
"alas," and refers to a combination of judgment
and sorrow, expressing righteous indignation. The
objects of woe are viewed as tragic figures. The
word "hypocrite" has its origins in Greek theater,
where it referred to a person who acts a part by
wearing a mask to cover his true person. The external show covers up the inward thoughts and
feelings of the person. The essence of hypocrisy is
described in verse 3, namely, the unwillingness to
conform to one's own expectations for others.

The first woe accuses the scribes and Pharisees
of shutting the kingdom of heaven to others even
while they themselves did not enter. This verse
has a parallel in Luke 11:52, where the scribes are
accused of taking away the key of knowledge and
not using it themselves. Presumably this refers to
a key of knowledge for entrance into the kingdom
of God, which would parallel the thought in verse
13. By their rejection of the teaching of John the
Baptist and the teaching of Jesus, the scribes and

Pharisees put the common people into a bind. Should they listen to these unsanctioned, unofficial, prophetic voices? Or should they heed the religious injunctions of the more established religious leaders? The language in verse 13 implies that some of the people were seeking to enter into the kingdom but were barred from doing so by the significant influence of the scribes and Pharisees.

The second woe is even more condemning than the first because it charges the scribes and Pharisees with seeking to convert others to their sect, which resulted in their also becoming sons of hell. The word "convert" used by Matthew refers to one who has approached or drawn near to the position of someone else. In their zeal to convince others of the rightness of their own approach to Judaism, the Pharisees literally did travel far distances (as we have seen in earlier sections of Matthew, where they were found in the extreme north and even in the Transjordan area). Why Jesus asserted that the convert would be twice as much a son of hell as the scribes and Pharisees is unclear. Perhaps it is because converts are sometimes the most fanatical of believers. If their belief is perverted, their life would be proportionately perverted.

The third woe is against the false dichotomy the Pharisees had set between important truth and less important truth. We have seen in our discussion of 5:33-37 that Jesus prohibited swearing or making vows in general, and specifically invoking

the name of something sacred, such as the temple
or the name of God, for one's oaths. In this case
Jesus called the Pharisees and scribes "blind
guides" and "blind fools." They were unable to
see the simple logic that swearing by the temple
instead of swearing by the gold of the temple did
not make one less obliged to fulfill one's vow. After all, the temple is more important than the gold
because it is the temple that makes the gold sanctified. Similarly, swearing by the altar is every bit
as onerous as swearing by the offering on the altar,
because it is the altar that makes the offering a
sanctified object. The same logic prevails with
verses 21 and 22. Barclay calls this special form of
casuistry "the science of evasion,"[2] implying that
the Pharisees made rules of language that would
enable them to escape the moral obligation of fulfilling their vows.

These three woes are condemnations of the
teachings of the Pharisees. Jesus asserted that in
regard to entrance into the kingdom of God, in regard to the essence of their Pharisaic religion and
their desire to bring converts into it and in regard
to their understanding of truth, the Pharisees were
blatantly wrong.

The fourth woe serves as a transition to the final three that expose the character of the Pharisees. We may also note at this transitional point
the variety of mental strategies Jesus used to at-
tack the hypocrisy of the Pharisees. For the first
woe, He used accusation. For the second woe, He
demonstrated a paradox. For the third woe, He

condemned them with His logic. For the fourth woe, He used biting humor. For the fifth and sixth woes, He used irony. And for the seventh woe, He used sarcasm.

Tithing one's earnings was expected of all Jews. It was not the tithing or even the scrupulous application of the principle that Jesus denounced. Rather, it was following the letter of the law fastidiously, even to the extreme of tithing condiments, while at the same time neglecting the broader principles of morality. Mint, dill and cumin were hardly the equivalents of justice, mercy and faithfulness on the moral scale. That should be most evident. Jesus did not discourage the principle of tithing but condemned the Pharisees and scribes for neglecting the more weighty aspects of religion. The humor He imposed uses the imagery of filtering a liquid to make it suitable for drinking. No doubt on many an occasion a Pharisee strained out a gnat from his drink, so the image would be familiar. Jesus accused them of being concerned about a gnat while at the same time swallowing a camel. In their concern about details, the scribes and Pharisees were neglecting what should be the obvious and significantly more important principles of true religion.

While the fourth woe suggests the Pharisees' preoccupation with cleanliness, the fifth woe addresses it directly. Jesus noted how anxious the Pharisees were when their food became ceremonially unclean through contact with an unclean utensil. Using this image, Jesus accused them of being preoccupied with external cleanliness but not worried about internal cleanliness. Robbery and self-indulgence were the contaminating influences on the inside. For the fifth time in this section, Jesus referred to the Pharisees and scribes as being blind (23:16, 17, 19, 24 and 26). Their inability to see spiritual truth ultimately led the Pharisees into their path of performance-based religion. In verse 26 Jesus wanted them to see the simple truth that inner cleanliness is far more important than external cleanliness.

Carrying this image of cleanliness one step further, in the sixth woe Jesus described the Pharisees and scribes as white-washed tombs, which appear beautiful on the outside but on the inside are contaminated with the foulness of dead corpses. For all Jews, to be near a tomb would jeopardize ceremonial cleanliness and make one ineligible for worship and other religious observances. By calling the Pharisees and scribes white-washed tombs, Jesus was stating as strongly as possible that their influence, far from being healthy and uplifting for other Jewish people, was contaminating and defiling.

Abandoning the imagery, Jesus then told them point blank that they appeared to be righteous people outwardly, but inwardly they were full of hypocrisy and lawlessness. The accusation of lawlessness must have stung even more than that of hypocrisy because the Pharisees fancied themselves to be the most law-oriented of all Jews. Jesus could make this assertion, how-

ever, with total believability because of the discussion in 22:37-40 where He" clearly stated
that the most important and encompassing laws
were the great principles of love for God and
love for other people. Far from drawing their
Jewish brothers and sisters closer to the true
faith of Israel, the Pharisees were contaminating
others, moving them farther from the true faith.

The seventh woe builds on the sixth woe with
the imagery of tombs. The scribes and Pharisees
had taken great pride in adorning the monuments
of the prophets and saints of old. By honoring
them in this way, the Pharisees and scribes were
trying to be identified with those great religious
figures of the past. Jesus turned their logic totally
upside-down by saying the fact that the scribes
and Pharisees embellished the tombs indicated
that they were ratifying the murdering of the
prophets and putting them in those tombs. Rather
than being identified with the righteous martyred
prophets, the Pharisees and scribes were more to
be identified with their fathers who were guilty of
murdering the prophets. Therefore, Jesus called
them a brood of vipers who deserved the sentence
of hell.

The scribes and Pharisees would also show
themselves to be sons of their murderous fathers
in the coming days as Jesus predicted. He would
be sending prophets, wise men and other scribes
whom the scribes and Pharisees would kill, crucify, scourge and persecute from city to city.
The idea here is that people who were truly in

tune with God and seeking to serve God in a pure way would not be tolerated by the scribes and Pharisees. By ratifying the martyrdom of former prophets, the scribes and Pharisees would be found guilty of "all the righteous blood that has been shed on earth" of all those who died seeking to be righteous in their walk before God. Jesus used severe irony in the command for them to fill up the measure of the guilt of their fathers (23:32), meaning, they should go ahead and do the same kind of activity, demonstrating that they are the moral as well as physical heirs of those who killed the prophets. Jesus was not exhorting them to do this, rather He was using irony to suggest that they would, in fact, do it and should know as they did it that Jesus had predicted that they would.

The repeated emphasis on the word "blood" in verse 35 was meant to shock the scribes and Pharisees to see their guiltiness before God in conspiring to kill Jesus. His righteous blood would stand in a line of succession that began with Abel, the first righteous man to be slain in Scripture, and continued to Zechariah, who was the last righteous man to be slain in the Old Testament (2 Chronicles 24:20-22).

With a final note of warning, Jesus mentioned that all these things would come upon "this generation" (Matthew 23:36). He was referring to the bloodguiltiness which they themselves would openly assume (see 27:25).

Lament over Jerusalem (Matthew 23:37-39)

Turning from direct address to the scribes and Pharisees, Jesus then gave a short lamentation over Jerusalem. He had just predicted in verse 34 that He would be sending prophets, wise men and scribes to Jerusalem who would be persecuted and killed. Now in His lamentation He referred to Jerusalem as the city who kills the prophets and stones those sent to her. Yet He yearned to care for Jerusalem. An image expressing tender care and protection was used by Jesus: He would have gathered the citizens under His protection as a mother hen gathers her chicks. But the citizens of Jerusalem were not willing. This passage indicates that Jesus was not a newcomer to Jerusalem. The Gospel of John indicates that Jesus traveled there on several occasions during His public ministry, whereas the synoptic Gospels give us only this instance of Jesus coming to Jerusalem. Certainly this phrase—of wanting often to gather her children together—indicates that Jesus came to Jerusalem more than once.

Part of His lamentation included a prophecy that Jerusalem was going to be destroyed. Her house would be left desolate or abandoned. The time would come, He said, when the Messiah would not be present and Jerusalem would be abandoned by her greatest prize. Not until He would come again would Jerusalem experience the blessing that she was now rejecting.

The Temple and Tribulation (Matthew 24:1-14)

Even today the view from the Mount of Olives looking west toward the city of Jerusalem is spectacular. It must have been even more so in the first century when Herod's temple was proudly prominent on Mount Zion. Herod's temple, the third in Israel's history, was built between the years 20 B.C. and 35 A.D. A magnificent structure, it covered one sixth of the property of Old Jerusalem. Some of its stones measured 40 feet long by 12 feet high by 18 feet wide. The alternating white and red coloring of the stones made the texture of the temple even more impressive.

The temple was the center of Jewish social, political and religious life. Far more significant than the White House to the United States, the Kremlin to Russia or the Houses of Parliament to England, the Jerusalem temple was the jewel of Israel.

This was the same temple in which Jesus was circumcised on His eighth day; where 12 years later He first confounded the scribes; and where Satan had taken Him to tempt Him to jump off. Likewise, it was the temple where He chased out the merchants, saying they had made it a den of robbers instead of a house of prayer. More recently He had silenced His opponents and their arguments in this very temple.

Having just lamented the future of Jerusalem and its demise, Jesus and His followers departed for the Mount of Olives. Perhaps understanding

His lamentation and seeing the wonder and beauty of the temple from their vantage point caused the disciples to speak in tones of reverence and awe about the great temple (24:1). Jesus took that opportunity to drive home the point He had been making about the future plight of Jerusalem by telling the disciples that the day was coming when not one stone of the temple would be left standing upon another. The destruction of the temple would be total.

Having arrived on the Mount of Olives, the disciples could no longer contain their curiosity about the future events Jesus talked about. They asked Him two questions, which to them may well have been one question: "When will this happen, and what will be the sign of your coming and of the end of the age?" (24:3). Their questions imply implicit trust in the words of Jesus and deep concern. Rather than answering the questions directly, Jesus took the opportunity to teach the disciples what their response should be to the events of the future.

The apocalyptic discourse found in Matthew 24, Mark 13 and Luke 21 must be understood first as a pastoral admonition to the followers of Jesus. He was more concerned to give His disciples guidance than illumination. He was not necessarily eager to unfold for them the mysteries of the future. Rather, as we will see, He was far more concerned to help the disciples be alert and confident, even amid the coming chaos. A key to unlocking the meaning of chapter 24 is seeing that the disciples did, in fact, ask Jesus two questions and that His response referred to two different eras. Trying to interpret this chapter to refer only to the future, that is, beyond the 20th century, will lead to great confusion. Much of what Jesus discussed with the disciples has already occurred in fulfillment of the events asked about in the first question, namely, when would the temple be destroyed.

Jewish people understood that a precursor to the end times was the coming of the Messiah. Jesus knew, even if the disciples did not, that as Messiah He was ushering in a messianic age that would be inserted between His two appearances. He warned the disciples not to be caught off guard about others who would come to claim messiahship. He wanted them to be confident that He was the Messiah, even though the end times were not necessarily upon them. As the future would show, people would embrace many false messiahs. We know of three from the book of Acts: Theudas (Acts 5:36), Judas of Galilee (5:37) and Simon (8:9). In fact these and others did mislead many.

Jesus then spoke about some events that are often considered to be signs of the end. To the contrary, He told the disciples that even though such things as wars, rumors of wars, persecutions, false prophets and lawlessness were coming, "the end is still to come. . . . All these are the beginning of birth pains" (Matthew 24:6-8).

Political, social and religious chaos would characterize the future, but these developments would not in themselves prefigure the end times. In fact, Jesus called for endurance on the part of the saved (v. 13), knowing that many would live through these events without experiencing the end times. The endurance is especially called for because Jesus told the disciples that they would be delivered over to tribulation; some would be killed, and many would be hated by all the nations because of their commitment to Jesus and His cause. Some would even fall away from following Him and turn on their former fellow disciples (24:9-10).

Jesus did give one positive sign about the end times. In verse 14 He told them that the good news about the kingdom of God would be proclaimed to the entire inhabited earth and only after that would the end come.[3]

Warning of Persecution (Matthew 24:15-28)

In verses 15-31 Jesus began to answer the two questions posed by the disciples. However, the interwovenness of His comments regarding "these things" (24:34) and "those days," that is, the end of the age (24:3, 29), can be very confusing. Two ideas may help us resolve this confusion. First, remember that Jesus was not trying to set out an eschatalogical timetable for the disciples. Rather, the force of His comments was pastoral in nature, encouraging the disciples to be on the alert for all that would take place. Second, even Jesus Himself did not know the precise time of His second coming (24:36).

Much of the confusion will be avoided if we understand that Jesus was talking about two eras, namely, the immediate generation of the first-century disciples (the events that would occur through the Roman persecution and the destruction of the temple), and the end times just prior to the second coming of Jesus. This distinction is made most clear by looking at verses 34 and 36. Certain events which Jesus referred to as "these things" would occur in the generation of the disciples (24:34). Other events that Jesus referred to as "that day" (24:36) would occur at a future time, the hour of which not even Jesus nor the angels of heaven knew for certain.

Verses 15-28 and verses 32-35 should be taken together, since they refer to the immediate generation of Jesus and the disciples. These two sections were the response of Jesus to the first question of the disciples about when these things would occur, meaning when the temple would be destroyed. The destruction of the temple would occur in conjunction with the abomination of desolation, which was prophesied in the book of Daniel.

In mentioning the abomination of desolation, Matthew adds parenthetically, "let the reader understand" (v. 15). Matthew wanted to make sure the readers understood the application, namely, that the events that occurred in the sack of Jerusalem and the destruction of the temple were the fulfillment of Daniel's prophecy. This event took place in A.D. 70 when Jerusalem finally fell to Titus and his army. The Jewish historian Josephus

states in his fifth book, *The War of the Jews*, that
97,000 people from Jerusalem were taken captive,
while 1,100,000 were either killed by the sword or
starved to death. The population of Jerusalem had
swelled because people crowded into the city from
all over the countryside. Josephus' description of
the war is exceedingly gruesome, depicting the
worst imaginable situation of death by disease,
cannibalism and starvation.

Anticipating this awfulness, Jesus very passion-
ately warned the disciples and whomever would
listen that they should not be in Jerusalem at that
time. Repeatedly He warned them to flee. Verses
16-21 speak of the urgency of such flight. Those in
Judea were warned to flee to the mountains; if
they were on the housetop or in the field, they
should not even retrieve their belongings, rather
they should move quickly to get out of Judea. Ad-
verse circumstances might hinder their flight,
such as pregnancy and motherhood, extremely
bad weather or even the Sabbath, when overly
scrupulous Jewish leaders might try to forbid
them from traveling.

The urgency of their flight from Jerusalem is
captured by the promise of the coming abomination of desolation. All Jewish people knew about
the event that took place in 170 B.C. when Antiochus Epiphanes, the king of Syria, captured Jerusalem and desecrated the temple by erecting an
altar to Zeus and sacrificing the flesh of swine
upon the altar. He turned the temple chambers
into public brothels and did everything he could

to desecrate the sacredness of the holy place of the
Jews. Jesus used the same imagery to speak about
the coming plunder of the temple. He referred to
this as a time of "great tribulation, such as has not
occurred since the beginning of the world until
now nor ever shall" (24:21, NASB).

Although the loss of life was enormous, the Roman siege of Jerusalem by ancient standards was
fairly short, lasting only four or five months. According to Josephus, Titus himself confessed that
if God had not been on the side of the Romans
they would not have been able to succeed as they
did. From a Christian perspective, interpreting the
words of Jesus in verses 13 and 22, we would understand that the physical deliverance of many in
Jerusalem was due to the presence of some of
God's elect, who, like in the days of Sodom when
as many as 10 righteous people could preserve the
city from God's judgment, were the cause for a reduced death toll. The exact historical event by
which Christians in Jerusalem or outside Jerusalem acted to shorten the siege is not specifically
known.

Another possible deterrent to fleeing from Jerusalem would be false messiahs coming on the
scene promising deliverance from the siege. Perhaps as in the days of Jeremiah, the inviolability of
the temple would be proclaimed, giving rise to
false hopes. Jesus sharply warned the disciples not
to listen to such false prophecy or to follow any
future so-called messiahs. The next time they
would see the Messiah would be in His second

coming when His appearance would be like the lightning that "comes from the east and flashes to the west."

Jesus then concluded this part of the discourse that referred to the immediate future by citing a proverbial saying about vultures gathering around a carcass. By this He was not referring to the literal corpses that would be the result of starvation due to the siege. Rather, He was speaking metaphorically about the false messiahs using this time of severe crisis for their own avaricious motives. Plummer notes, "There may also be a reference to God's judgments coming upon a corrupt state of society, and (as a special illustration of this principle) the Romans coming on the Jewish Church and nation."[4]

Return of the Son of Man (Matthew 24:29-31)

Although the previous section referred mostly to the present generation of disciples, the warning of Jesus about false messiahs prompted Him in verse 27 to give an insight about the appearance of His second coming. It is to that verse that verse 29 must refer. Immediately after the tribulation of "those days" refers to the coming of the Son of man (v. 27). We are not to understand that Jesus or Matthew expected that the coming of the Son of Man would immediately succeed the great tribulation of the first century. Verses 29-31 speak to the second part of the disciples' question, namely, ". . . what [would] be the sign of [Jesus'] coming and of the end of the age?" Jewish literature referred often to "the Day of the LORD," using apocalyptic language such as in these three verses. The darkening of the sun and the moon and the falling of the stars from the sky were often interpreted metaphorically to coincide with the phrase "the heavenly bodies will be shaken." Perhaps these apocalyptic phrases refer not to the literal bodies of the heavens but to all other universal powers that would pretend to compete with the Son of Man. His brilliance, upon His return, will be so great that all lesser lights will be extinguished or not visible. We need not, however, necessarily interpret these phrases metaphorically because, to be sure, the brilliance of His appearance will be so overwhelming (such as lightning, 24:27) that in that moment no other light from the sky could possibly be visible.

This coming of the Son of Man will not occur until all the nations of the earth have had a witness about His identity (24:14); therefore, when the nations of the earth do witness His coming, those who have been unbelieving will indeed mourn as is stated in verse 30. Their mourning will be due to their unbelief and what they know will be the consequences of it. The Son of Man will at that time gather together His elect from all over the earth and draw them to Himself. This third reference to the elect (24:22, 24, 31) makes it abundantly clear that only the ones the Messiah called to follow Him and who remained true to Him (see 24:10-11, 24) would be blessed by His return.

The Parable of the Fig Tree (Matthew 24:32-41)

This section of the apocalyptic discourse can be extremely confusing unless we take very seriously and use vigorously the language that has been our guide through this passage. The distinction between "these things" found in verse 34, and "that day," found in verse 36, is exceedingly important.

"These things" (notice 24: 3, 8, 33-34) refer to the immediate generation when Jerusalem would be sacked, the temple destroyed and great tribulation experienced. For this interpretation to be correct, the pronoun in verse 33 must be "it," namely, "it is near, right at the door" (NIV), not, "he," as found in the NASV. The pronoun refers to the siege of Jerusalem.

Jesus used the illustration of a fig tree to help the disciples understand that when they saw the events corresponding to "these things" mentioned in verses 5-28, they would understand that the great cataclysmic event of their age was about to occur. Jesus affirmed that these things would take place within their own generation (v. 34). He assured them with the proverbial statement that heaven and earth would pass away, but His words would certainly not pass away.

Verse 36 then speaks of "that day," namely, the day of His return and the end of the age, which was the content of the second part of the question the disciples asked in verse 3. "That day" will be attended by cosmic upheaval spoken of in verses

29-31 and verses 37-41. The coming of the Son of
man will occur in an era similar to the pre-Noahic
days when people were unaware that an impend-
ing disaster was looming. The coming of the Son
of Man will be a great surprise to the nations. The
use of the word "coming" is interesting in Matthew 24; it is the Greek word *parousia* which is
found in the Gospels only in this chapter (24: 3,
27, 37, 39). The phrase "second coming" does not
occur in Scripture but certainly is drawn from this
particular word.

On the occasion of the coming of the Son of
Man the human family will experience separation.
The force of verses 40 and 41, however, should
not be so much on the separation, but on the fact
that people will be going about their daily business, such as working in the field or grinding at
the mill, when history will suddenly be inter-
rupted.

Warning to be Ready (Matthew 24:42-51)

For both the first generation of the Christian era
and the last generation yet to come, the warning
to be ready sounded by Jesus was and is and will
be appropriate. Because the time of His appearing
is unknown, His people should always be expect-
ing Him. Just as people who knew in advance that
their home was going to be broken into would
take every precaution, even so those who know
history and the world will be broken into by the
coming of the Lord must also constantly be in a
state of readiness. Verse 44 emphatically declares

that the coming of the Son of Man will be a total surprise. There are no specific signs that will precede that appearance, unlike the signs that preceded the ransacking of Jerusalem. The only condition that must precede the coming of the Son of Man is that already referred to in verse 14, namely, the spread of the gospel around the world so that all nations will have had opportunity to accept the reality and identity of the Messiah.

Jesus drew one practical conclusion from this entire apocalyptic discourse. His people are like stewards who know that their master will come but who do not know when he will come. A faithful and sensible steward will constantly be doing the work assigned to him by the master so that when the master returns, he is found to be faithful. His reward will certainly be given by the master. Jesus told His disciples not to be like an evil steward who would exploit the master's absence by being cruel and selfish. That steward will be surprised by the return of the master and appropriately punished. There is no reason for fearful and hysterical expectation of the Son of Man for those who are faithful in serving Him as He has prescribed, but there is every reason for alertness and faithful, obedient living so that it does not matter when the master will come. All of life is to be lived in anticipation of His coming.

The Parable of Ten Virgins (Matthew 25:1-13)

We have just seen at the end of chapter 24 that Jesus admonished His disciples to continue watching and working as they awaited the coming events. Those two themes, watching and working, are now illustrated in two parables and an extended vision of judgment.

Any teller of a parable has the right to create the story as he chooses. A good parable has at least two features: (1) resonance with reality, that is, the situation is believable because it reflects real life, and (2) an obvious connection between the story and the lesson to be learned. The parable of the 10 virgins may seem to lack the former in that the circumstances seem quite remote from the norms of our culture. William Barclay, however, assures us that the events in the parable are perfectly true to life in the first century.[5]

Without going into the details of first-century nuptial customs we may note that the 10 maidens were to be attendants to the bride. In this parable the bride is not mentioned because she is not required for the purposes of the story. It was the duty of the bride's attendants to remain on alert for the coming of the bridegroom for his bride. Whereas normally the bride represents the church, in this parable the bride's attendants represent the visible church. Some of them were found to be prepared for the coming of the bridegroom; others were not. The lamps of the maidens represent the attitude of expectancy. While all 10 theoretically expected the coming of the bridegroom, only five were truly prepared. The two obvious lessons that spring from this parable are that the coming of the bridegroom is so important that preparation should not be postponed to the last minute. Secondly the parable teaches that one person's preparation cannot atone for the lack of preparation of another. Consistent with His admonitions in the previous chapter, Jesus emphasized in this poignant way the extreme importance of watchful and wise expectancy as disciples await the reappearance of the Messiah.

The immediate significance of the parable was directed against the Jews who as the chosen people of God were presumably spending their entire history awaiting the Messiah. The fact that many of them were unprepared for Him when He came must be viewed as a great tragedy.

The Buried Talent (Matthew 25:14-30)

Not only must the servants of Christ be wise, as taught in the parable of the 10 virgins, but they must also be faithful, as taught in the parable of the talents. In this story three servants are entrusted with different amounts of money. Attention should not be on the different amounts apart from the fact that perhaps the one who failed viewed his talents to be of such minimal value that he became slothful. The primary point of the parable is that, whatever amount of gifts have been entrusted to a servant, the master requires a diligent use of those gifts and expects a tangible return. The parable implies strongly that besides waiting expectantly for the master, wise stewards will be found serving faithfully as they wait. The reward given to those who serve faithfully and present the master with a return on his investment is the opportunity for greater service and responsibility. The laziness and imprudence of the unfaithful servant results in all opportunity being withheld from him. Furthermore, the lazy servant receives the severest punishment possible (25:30). The severity of the judgment on the unfaithful servant is due to the fact that he knew the nature of his master and still went out and hid the talent in the ground (25:24-25). The master reminded him that he could have been just as lazy and still have presented a profit to the master by investing the money in a bank. Omission even of this simple activity indicated clearly to the master that the servant had absolutely no interest in being a benefit to the master's estate. Faithfulness in service requires a passionate interest in serving the master using whatever talents one has been given.

The Sheep and the Goats (Matthew 25:31-46)

While we may interpret the former two parables as rebukes to the Jewish people because of their insensitivity to the Messiah's first coming, the sequel indicates quite clearly that Jesus also had the future in mind. This section of Scripture affirms not only the second coming of Jesus, but consistent with the language in First Thessalonians and in Revelation, He is envisioned as a glorified Conqueror. His coming will be in glory, surrounded by angels. He will be sitting on a glorious throne with all nations before Him (25:31-32).

The emphasis of this section is on judgment. Verses 32 and 33 use the imagery of a shepherd separating sheep from goats. Similar to the imagery found in two parables of the kingdom (Matthew 13:24-30, 47-50), this teaching distinguishes between two categories. The obvious conclusion to draw is that judgment entails a process of separation, whether wheat from tares, good fish from bad fish or sheep from goats.

In verse 34 the picture changes from a pastoral scene to the royal throne. Those who have been separated and put to the right of the king are welcomed into the kingdom. Thus far there are no surprises in this scenario. The next six verses, however, add new insight into the concept of the judgment. The king, speaking of his corporate citizenry, commends these who "are blessed by my Father" because "I was hungry . . . thirsty . . . a stranger . . . needed . . . sick . . . and in prison." In each case these who are welcomed into the kingdom had ministered to him supplying what was needed (food, drink, hospitality, clothes, visitation). The righteous are surprised to hear these comments, not knowing when they rendered such ministry to him. The king's response shows that he was speaking corporately by saying that as they rendered such ministry to "one of the least of these brothers of mine," they ministered also to him.

Contrariwise, those who were separated and put to the left (the goats), the king banished from his presence, calling them "accursed ones" sending

them to "the eternal fire you who are cursed prepared for the devil and his angels." His rationale
for this severe judgment was that these accursed
ones failed to render ministry "for one of the least
of these," meaning his brethren. Verse 46 sums up
the destiny of these two groups by saying that the
latter group will go away into eternal punishment,
whereas the righteous will inherit eternal life.

Looking superficially at the passage, we might
be tempted to see a strong element of social gospel
here. We might assume that the judgment is going
to be based entirely on the works that one rendered or did not render. Some have interpreted
this passage that way. It must be noted, however,
that the beings who were judged were already of
entirely different status from one another prior to
the judgment. Some were sheep, some were goats.
It ought not be presumed that their ministering or
failing to minister to the brethren of the king determined whether they would be sheep or goats.
Rather, the ministry of those who already were
sheep was positive and compassionate. The failure
to minister by the goats indicated their lack of
compassion. To be true to other Scripture we
must interpret the passage with the understanding
that the social activity rendered or not rendered
did not determine the outcome of these righteous
and accursed individuals. Their destiny was already determined when they became sheep or
goats. The goats are the ones who have rejected
the Messiah and have paid no attention to the people of the Messiah. The sheep are those who, by

ministering to the people of the Messiah, demonstrate that they are already part of that kingdom.

One other interesting distinction found in this passage is the intended purposes of the places of destiny. Those who are righteous inherit "the kingdom prepared for you since the creation of the world" (25:34). Those who are condemned, however, are sent away into eternal punishment "into the eternal fire which has been prepared for the devil and his angels" (25:41). The kingdom has been prepared for people, whereas the place of punishment has been prepared for the devil and his angels. The fact that people are sent to the place of punishment is further evidence of their rejection of the Messiah which necessarily implies their coalition with the enemy of the Messiah.

The fifth discourse ends abruptly with the statement about the two possible destinies. Overshadowing this entire discourse was the harsh condemnation of Jesus against the Pharisees. We saw it in the woes of chapter 23. We saw it in the parable of the fig tree in chapter 24. And we saw it in the two parables in chapter 25, as well as in this last section about judgment. We ought to note that the primary audience of this entire discourse is the disciples (vv. 23:1, 24:3). Jesus wanted them to understand fully that His kingdom should not be understood merely as another conservative Judaic sect. So intensely spiritual and openly irreligious is the tenor of this discourse that the disciples would know prior to moving into the passion experiences that, whatever may come, the cause to which they were committed was decidedly unorthodox and compellingly heavenly.

Endnotes

1. Alfred Plummer, *An Exegetical Commentary on The Gospel According to St. Matthew* (Grand Rapids: Baker Book House, 1982), p. 316.
2. William Barclay, *The Gospel of Matthew*, Vol. 2 (Philadelphia: The Westminster Press, 1958), p. 323.
3. Because much of the readership of this commentary may well be affiliated with The Christian and Missionary Alliance, we ought not pass Matthew 24:14 without recognizing its special significance. This was a favorite text of Dr. A.B. Simpson because of its eschatalogical significance as well as its missiological significance. For Dr. Simpson, the passion for global evangelization arose not only out of his burden for the lost, but more so out of his passion for the return of Jesus. He assumed that the second coming of Jesus would be in conjunction with the end. That being the case, prior to the coming of Jesus the gospel must obviously be proclaimed to all people groups throughout the entire world. Simpson and others believed this task could be done in their own generation if enough people were committed to worldwide missionary evangelization. Although the task was not completed in his day, the advance of the cause of missions was greatly accelerated and many missionary

denominations and organizations trace their roots back to the last 30 years of the 19th century.

4. Plummer, p. 335.
5. Barclay, p. 353.

CHAPTER 11

The Execution and Triumph of the King

Matthew 26-28

The curtain rises on the final act of this intense drama. The previous narrative section (Matthew 19-22) was filled with conflict. Ten times in four chapters we saw the enemies of Jesus manipulating and maneuvering to find Jesus guilty of some prosecutable offense. Consistently He beat them at their own game, showing that they were in reality the ones who were most guilty of disregarding their own religion. Nevertheless, Jesus knew that despite their failure in argumentation, the Jewish leaders would ultimately find a way to put Him to death. This was part of God's plan for Jesus. And the final three chapters of Matthew's Gospel describe in much detail the process and the ordeal through which Jesus was to experience the cross, the grave and the resurrection.

Matthew 26:1 begins with an end-of-discourse formula similar to those we have seen before, using the words, "When Jesus had finished saying all these things." On this occasion He uttered His final prediction about His coming passion and His precise knowledge of the timing of the crucifixion. The key verb in the passion prediction in verse 2 is "handed over" ("betrayed," KJV). This verb may refer to the act of the betrayer who takes center stage in the next several paragraphs (26: 6-25), or it may refer to being delivered up according to the purpose and foreknowledge of God (see Acts 2:23).

Matthew then describes the setting for the plot to fulfill the execution of Jesus. We are not surprised to find that the main players are those who have been challenging Jesus throughout the Gospel. The chief priests and elders gathered together in the court of Caiaphas the High Priest. In their plotting they decided to avoid unnecessary public attention and were hoping to wait until after Passover. The plan was to seize Jesus "in some sly way" (or "by subtility," KJV)), indicating that the Jewish leaders were trying to remove Jesus from the scene in a quiet way. Their plan was changed by the unexpected offer of Judas, which enabled them to move forward with their plan by having an insider close to Jesus fully cooperate with them.

Matthew's Details and Major Themes

Before moving further into the passion story,

we must not miss the opportunity to notice the tremendously valuable contribution Matthew's Gospel makes to our understanding of the passion of Jesus. Many details not found in the other three Gospels are supplied by Matthew. Rather than calling attention to them as they occur throughout the commentary on this section, we will list them here comprehensively:

26:15	thirty pieces of silver
26:25	Judas saying, "Rabbi, is it I?"
26:52-54	"Put away your sword"
26:59	"false" witnesses
26:63	Caiaphas saying, "I charge you under oath"
26:65	"He has spoken blasphemy"
27:3-10	description of the death of Judas
27:19	the message of Pilate's wife
27:24-25	Pilate's washing his hands
27:51-53	earthquake, open tombs, dead saints walking
27:62-66	posting of the Jewish guard
28:2-4	earthquake and description of angel
28:9-10	Jesus appears to two Marys
28:11-15	report of the guard
28:16-20	appearance in Galilee and "Great Commission"

Besides the unique passion material, Matthew's account of the passion contains several major themes that ought to be noticed. His peculiar casting of the characters is noteworthy. The disciples are seen to be uncertain, a bit out of touch, rather weak although well intentioned. Jesus appears to be in total control, very human, but extremely courageous, passive to the abuse He suffered and fully vindicated. The Romans are seen to be accomplices to a Jewish plot, rather barbaric and coarse in their treatment of Jesus, certainly confused by what was happening and almost reluctant as participants. The scribes and Pharisees, along with the chief priests and Caiaphas, are seen to be cool, dishonest, hypocritical and fearful to the point of paranoia.

As has been the case throughout his Gospel, Matthew also supplies references to the fulfillment of Old Testament passages. In 26:24 Jesus declared that the Son of Man is to go "just as it is written about him." He quoted Zechariah 13:7 in Matthew 26:31 referring to the striking of the shepherd and the scattering of the sheep. As part of His rebuke to Peter's overzealous defense, Jesus mentioned in 26:54 that the Scriptures had to be fulfilled in this particular way. Likewise, in verse 56 Jesus said all this has taken place "that the writings of the prophets might be fulfilled." And then in 27:9-10 Matthew reports the fulfillment of the Old Testament prophecy about the 30 pieces of silver being used to buy a potter's field.

Furthermore, Matthew provides continued emphasis on Peter in this section. In 26:33-35 Peter declares that he personally would never abandon Jesus, even though everyone else would. In 26:37 Peter is one of the three who attended Jesus in Gethsemane. Notice that Jesus' disapproval of the three was directed to Peter specifically (26:40). In 26:58 Peter followed Jesus at a distance, and

26:69-75 describes Peter's great denial of Jesus.

The Bethany Anointing (Matthew 26:6-19)

Matthew's account of the anointing of Jesus in Bethany is rather restrained. We know from John's Gospel that the woman who anointed Jesus was Mary, the sister of Martha and Lazarus (John 12:1-3). Furthermore, Matthew withholds the name of the disciple who took the lead in censoring Mary for her extravagance, attributing it generally to the disciples (26:8). John specifically mentions that Judas was the offended disciple. Perhaps some of the other disciples sympathized with this short-sighted sense of stewardship, so that Matthew spread the blame onto them as well. Furthermore, Matthew does not indicate the tremendous value of the vial of perfume (more than 300 denarii)—a year's wages.

Luke's Gospel reports a similar incident (7:36-50), but its differences are enough to warrant the assumption that Luke reported a separate incident. In both cases, however, Jesus gladly received this ministry of compassion that others felt was extravagant. The disciples considered the use of the perfume to be a waste. In normal situations perhaps Jesus might have agreed, but in this case He considered it to be a "beautiful thing" (26:10). To be sure, the disciples had learned well the lesson from Jesus about concern for the poor, but in this instance the Master wanted the disciples to understand the issue of priority (26:11).

Whether or not Mary understood the full impli-

cations of her extravagant act, Jesus indicated that
the anointing was in preparation for His burial.
Generally, anointing was used for one of three
purposes: (1) a prostitute would anoint one of her
customers as part of her immoral service; (2) a
designated leader would be anointed for recognition of his special status; or (3) a corpse would be
anointed as part of the burial ritual. Obviously it
was the third purpose that Mary had in mind, and
perhaps she among all the followers of Jesus most
clearly understood and believed the passion predictions of Jesus. The fact that we continue to re-
tell this remarkable incident after nearly 2,000
years verifies the truthfulness of verse 13.

The word "then" with which verse 14 begins
seems to indicate that the activity of Judas was a
sequel and partially caused by the previous event,
namely, the use of the perfume. John's Gospel
makes it patently clear that Judas was particularly
offended by Mary's act. We must not suppose that
the Jewish leaders had at this point put a bounty
on the head of Jesus, but it may have been well
known that they were hostile to Jesus and eager to
find a way to remove Him from society. Whatever
his true motives may have been, Judas used this
opportunity to conspire with the enemies of Jesus.
He found a receptive group of chief priests, bar-
gained with them and was paid 30 pieces of silver
on the spot.

Much debate surrounds the exact chronology of
the last few days of Jesus' life. Plummer suggests
that "it is best to hold fast to the very clear and

thoroughly consistent statements in the Fourth Gospel. . . ."[1] Knowing that He would not be able to celebrate Passover on Friday evening, Jesus wanted to celebrate it ahead of time and ordered the disciples to find the place for preparing the meal. He indicated the way that they would find the proper location, and the disciples did exactly as Jesus ordered, as is described more fully in Matthew than the other synoptic Gospels.

The Passover Supper (Matthew 26:20-35)

On the Thursday evening before His death, Jesus and His 12 disciples entered the room that had been prepared for the observance of Passover. In typical Middle Eastern style, they reclined at the table, and with great solemnity Jesus uttered that one of the Twelve would betray Him. In oriental settings it was unheard of to eat bread with a man while contemplating a hostile and treacherous act, such as betrayal. Yet the disciples did not dispute Jesus, but looked inwardly, searching their own souls as to whether they would be the one. Judas appears not to have been suspected at this point. The comment by Jesus that one who dipped his hand with Him into the bowl would be the betrayer was not an indication that the betrayer would be Judas; rather, it was a reaffirmation of the enormity of the treachery that one who could share such intimate fellowship with Him would be His betrayer. Most likely there was only one dish into which each of the disciples was dipping his bread, so each of them was a possible suspect at this point. Mark and Luke both withhold the identification of Judas in this incident, whereas John and Matthew both expose Judas. According to John, Jesus secretly revealed the information, probably to the beloved disciple himself (John 13:24-26). Matthew indicated that Judas himself asked whether it was he and Jesus affirmed it to him by saying, "Yes, it is you" (Matthew 26:25). At that time Judas may have removed himself from their company (see John 13:30).

During the eating of the Passover meal, Jesus established a strong connection between the bread and His body, and the wine and His blood. The phrases "this is my body" (26:26) and "this is my blood of the covenant" (26:28) have been the center of great debate over the centuries. The Greek word for "is" is not emphatic, and perhaps would not have even been expressed in the Aramaic language, which was undoubtedly used by our Lord here. Plummer notes that the choice of interpretation lies between two options, namely, "this represents My Body" and "this is . . . identified with My Body."[2]   In a footnote Plummer shows that Jesus frequently used metaphors to refer to His person, for example, "I am the door," "I am the true vine," "I am the light of the world."[3]

The Roman Catholic doctrine of transubstantiation, in which it is believed that through the blessing of the elements the bread and wine are literally and mystically turned into the material body and blood of Jesus, is based on a literal understanding of these phrases and sayings such as, "unless you eat the flesh of the Son of Man and drink His blood, you have no life in you," and "For my flesh is real food and my blood is real drink" (John 6:53, 55). Even these verses, however, have been clearly understood to be metaphorical by most interpreters. Of the four renderings of the eucharistic words (Matthew 26:26-28; Mark 14:22-24; Luke 22:19-20; 1 Corinthians 11:24-25), Matthew's is unique in two ways. Only in Matthew did Jesus command that all of the disciples should drink from the cup, and only in Matthew is there a reference to the remission of sins. Unlike the eucharistic words in Luke and First Corinthians, neither Matthew nor Mark contains a command to continue the celebration of the ritual in remembrance of Christ.

Verse 29, in which Jesus indicated He would no longer drink from the fruit of the vine until the coming of the kingdom, should be understood to be a formal farewell, as well as a statement of eschatalogical expectation. We might be surprised to hear that there will be eating and drinking in the kingdom, but we need to remember the Jewish idea about the kingdom being a banquet (Isaiah 25:6; Luke 13:29; 14:15; 22:30; Revelation 3:20; 19:9). That joyous reunion is the hope Jesus offers His kingdom community.

Concluding the meal with a hymn, which no doubt was the second part of the *Hallel* (Psalms 115-118), Jesus and the disciples left the room and headed out of Jerusalem on the east side toward the Mount of Olives. During their travel Jesus in-

dicated that during that very night all the disciples
would abandon Him in fulfillment of Zechariah
13:7. Anticipating scattering of the disciples, Jesus
promised that after He was raised from the dead
He would meet them again in Galilee. Peter, with
great confidence, stated that even though all the
others might abandon Jesus, he would not. In fact
after Jesus affirmed that Peter would deny Him
three times on that very night, Peter insisted that
he was ready to die with Jesus rather than deny
Him. The other disciples apparently joined in the
same chorus and Jesus was content to let the ensuing hours demonstrate the reality of His statement.

The Garden Prayer and Arrest (Matthew 26:36-56)

Arriving at the garden called Gethsemane with
His disciples, Jesus instructed them to sit while
He went to pray. Then He took Peter, James and
John with Him into the garden. His desire was for
them to remain with Him, keeping watch during
what He knew would be a time of great travail of
soul. His deep grief is indicated by falling on His
face to pray that God would remove the cup from
Him if it were at all possible (Matthew 26:37-39).
Although Jesus knew that it was not possible, that,
indeed, it was for this very hour that He came to
the world, His prayer ought not to be considered
insincere. Clearly the shadow of death hovering
over Him sent a chill through His soul that caused
even Jesus to want to be rid of the prospect of

such an unjust and grisly death. The resignation of His will to the Father's (v. 39) ensured that He would endure the awful torture associated with His crucifixion.

While the deep grief of Jesus is clearly a focus of this passage, Matthew's purpose for reporting it seems to center more on the disciples and their failure to minister to Jesus during this time. The phrase in verse 41 about the spirit being willing but the flesh being weak may well have been a common saying. Jesus linked the saying to the importance of remaining watchful and prayerful to avoid falling into temptation. Matthew shows how Jesus engaged in His deep prayer on three occasions that night, and in each case the disciples were unable to refrain from sleeping.

More saddened than angered, Jesus, upon completing His praying, reproved the disciples for their sleeping and then told them it was now time to meet His betrayer. Perhaps He could see lights or hear voices of those who were ascending the Mount of Olives. He certainly knew the purpose of the intrusion into the garden, namely, His being seized and arrested. The inappropriate signal used by Judas to indicate which man was Jesus was staged to overcome the possibility of mistaken identity during the darkness of the hours. Nevertheless, as Judas hailed Jesus as Rabbi and kissed Him, Jesus said, "Friend, do what you came for."

At that moment, Peter, perhaps out of embarrassment for his lack of alertness and out of an inappropriate sense of bravado in fulfilling his earlier vows, drew out his sword as if to fight the cohort of soldiers. A cohort was 600 foot soldiers. His only victim, however, was the high priest's slave whose ear Peter cut off. Luke indicates that Jesus proceeded to touch the ear of the stricken man and healed him (Luke 22:51). The inappropriateness of Peter's zeal was expressed by Jesus telling him and all that care to heed that "all who draw the sword will die by the sword" (Matthew 26:52).

Jesus then reminded His immediate audience that these events were a fulfillment of the Scriptures. After turning to the soldiers, Jesus expressed an amazement that they came for Him as a fugitive from justice, reminding them that He was often with them in the temple teaching them, and they had many opportunities to seize Him. If escaping the danger of their company were His desire, He surely would have used greater caution in the earlier days. Again He reminded them that their activity was in accord with prophetic Scriptures. Verse 56 ends with the statement that all the disciples then left Jesus and fled.

The Trial and Denial (Matthew 26:57-75)

An analysis of all four Gospels reveals that during the early morning hours Jesus endured six interviews or trials with various officials. On two occasions He was examined by Caiaphas, the high priest. Once Annas, a former high priest, interviewed Jesus. Caiaphas sent Jesus to Herod for examination. And twice Pontius Pilate tried Jesus.

The first stop was the home of Caiaphas where the high priests, scribes and elders who formed the Sanhedrin were gathered. Knowing that Jesus was not guilty of a crime worthy of execution, the council kept trying to formulate a charge based on false testimony that would render Jesus worthy of death. Two false witnesses agreed that Jesus said He would destroy the temple and rebuild it in three days. The closest reference to a statement like this was when Jesus told the Jewish leaders that if they destroyed the temple of His body, in three days He would raise it up (John 2:19). Why Caiaphas considered this charge to be worthy of further examination is rather puzzling since the Romans would not take it seriously. Nevertheless, he hounded Jesus by trying to get Him to incriminate Himself by declaring that He was the Messiah, the Son of God (Matthew 26:63).

We ought to note that in many ways this trial was totally illegal. First, the trial should not have been held at the home of Caiaphas, but convened in the usual hall of the Sanhedrin. Second, trying to obtain false testimony was certainly against the judicial principles of the Sanhedrin. Furthermore, the president of the Sanhedrin, Caiaphas, was not acting legitimately by trying to get Jesus to incriminate Himself. Verse 63 indicates a desperation in Caiaphas' voice as he appealed to the name of God, thinking Jesus would respond. About this he was correct. Jesus replied, "Yes, it is as you say," (similar to Jesus' statement to Judas in 26:25). Jesus then stated that as Son of Man, He

would be witnessed "sitting at the right hand of
the Mighty One and coming on the clouds of
heaven" (26:64). Plummer notes:

> These two verses (63, 64) are of great im-
> port. They introduce a great change in
> Christ's method. Just as He had taken great
> pains to avoid premature capture, and im-
> prisonment, and death, by retiring before
> His enemies, avoiding dangerous regions,
> and keeping His movement secret, *until* the
> hour for His passion had come; so also as
> part of this method, He had been very re-
> served about His own personality, and had
> avoided premature disclosure of the fact that
> He was the Messiah. . . . But now there is no
> need of reserve any longer. He is challenged
> by the highest religious authority in the Su-
> preme Council of the nation to declare him-
> self; and for the first time He declares
> publicly that He whom they are determined
> to condemn to death is the Messiah.[4]

This reference to Daniel 7:13 by Jesus was understood by the high priest exactly as Jesus had intended. Using a symbol of outrage by tearing his
clothes, Caiaphas declared Jesus to be guilty of
blasphemy and did not even give the Sanhedrin
members their normal opportunity for individual
response to the charges, starting with the youngest
and proceeding to the oldest. Rather, as a group
they were forced to declare Jesus' guilt.

The uncivil treatment of Jesus after the verbal condemnation is still somewhat surprising, even though we have earlier seen the pitiable character displayed by some of the religious leaders. They began beating Him, spitting on Him and taunting Him by saying that as Messiah He should be able to prophesy who was hitting Him.

Matthew 26:58 indicates that Peter had followed Jesus and His captors at a distance, all the way to the courtyard of the high priest. Verse 69 turns the focus back upon Peter, who was identified by a servant girl as being one who had been with Jesus the Galilean. Peter's first denial was a simple lie. Knowing that he was in danger, Peter withdrew himself toward the gate of the courtyard, but then another servant girl saw and also identified him. With an oath, Peter denied knowing Jesus, giving greater vehemence to his denial. Before long, others contradicted Peter, noting that his Galilean accent identified him as one who was with Jesus. Peter then began to curse and swear in his denial. At that point the rooster crowed, verifying Jesus' prediction about Peter's denial. After Peter remembered Jesus' statement about the rooster crowing, he went out and wept bitterly. Peter's own self-confidence and his lack of alertness were his undoing. His courage in the garden and even in following Jesus to the high priest's courtyard indicate his intention to remain true to his earlier promise. In the obviously dangerous moment of the arrest, Peter had braced himself for an act of heroism. Now, however, in a seemingly

less dangerous moment, Peter was unable to remain true to his own desire.

Judas' Suicide (Matthew 27:1-10)

As dawn broke, the Sanhedrin members met a
second time to formally charge Jesus with blasphemy and conspired to have Him put to death.
Knowing that under Roman law they could not
execute Him, they delivered Him up to Pilate, the
governor of the land. Having their will accomplished was not an easy matter, as we will see
presently. Matthew breaks the drama by moving
the spotlight to Judas to see what would become
of him. Unlike John, who believed Judas was motivated by money in betraying Jesus, Matthew
pictures Judas as one who was depressed about
the outcome of his action. Verse 3 indicates that
when he saw Jesus was condemned, he felt re-
morse and tried to return the money to the enemies of Jesus. Verse 3 indicates he was trying to
repent of betraying innocent blood, but the chief
priests and elders were completely unconcerned
about Judas or about his testimony regarding Jesus' innocence. Throwing the pieces of silver into
the sanctuary, Judas departed and hanged himself.

If money was not Judas' motive, and if he knew
Jesus was innocent, we might well wonder why
Judas betrayed Jesus. Doubtlessly, the most sensible explanation is that as a Zealot, Judas was eager
to see the overthrow of the Roman occupation.
Knowing that Jesus had enough power to put
down His enemies, Judas may have been putting

Jesus in a position that would have forced Him to destroy the Romans. However, had this been the motive, we would have expected Judas to continue watching the drama to see whether Jesus would take action against the Romans. Rather, his suicide came shortly after his public declaration of guilt.

The details regarding Judas' death found in 27:5-10 differ slightly from information provided by Luke in Acts 1:18-20. Both accounts, however, indicate that the betrayer came to a violent end, that a field was bought with the blood money, and that it was subsequently named "Field of Blood." Characteristically, Matthew indicates that what had happened was the fulfillment of prophecy. Matthew 27:9-10 seems to be a rendering of Zechariah 11:12-13, although Matthew attributes these ideas to Jeremiah, the closest references being Jeremiah 18:2-12, 19:1-13, and perhaps 32:6-9.

The Roman Trial (Matthew 27:11-32)

Matthew compresses the drama of the Roman trial somewhat, but gives the essential information. As procurator of Judea, Pilate resided in Caesarea but was now in Jerusalem to ensure tranquillity during the days of Passover when the population of the city would have increased sixfold. The members of the Sanhedrin, knowing that their charge of blasphemy against Jesus would mean little to the Roman government, changed the charge to sedition, an offense that any Roman governor would have to take seriously.

Having heard perhaps of the triumphal entry of

Jesus into Jerusalem a few days earlier, Pilate gave initial credence to their charge. Therefore, he asked Jesus outright whether He considered Himself to be King of the Jews. Jesus' response may be understood in several ways, but certainly it was not a denial that He was a king of the Jews in some way. John's Gospel supplies information that helps make the ongoing drama more realistic. Jesus stated that His kingdom was not of this world. Pilate, already believing the Jews to be a rather odd group, would have understood that before him was not a seditious and dangerous political enemy, but rather a pathetic victim of the fanatical displeasure of the Jewish leadership. It is quite clear in Matthew and the other Gospels that Pilate did not believe that by Roman law Jesus was worthy of death.

Plummer makes the interesting observation that our Lord's behavior to Pilate in private was quite different than it was before the Jewish hierarchy in public. With Pilate He was very direct and free in His responses, whereas, once Jesus stood before the false accusers, He refused to cooperate, as a protest against the unrighteousness of their activity. The silence of Jesus in front of His accusers amazed Pilate (Matthew 27:13-14).

Pilate, no doubt, was quite pleased to find that he had a way out of this predicament. Each year, as a gesture of goodwill, the governor released a prisoner during the Passover Feast. A notorious seditionist named Barabbas, who had been accused of murder and was destined to be executed, was put forward by Pilate in contrast to Jesus. The governor asked the crowd which of the two they would prefer to see released, thinking, of course, that the harmless Galilean would be released rather than the murderous Zealot.

Verse 19, which is unique to Matthew, shows that the wife of the Roman governor sent a message to her husband warning him not to be involved unjustly against "that innocent man" because during the night she had suffered greatly in a dream because of Him. Undoubtedly at this point Pilate expected that he would be able to respect his wife's admonition. But such was not to be the case. As he continued to press the possibility of releasing Jesus while retaining Barabbas, Pilate was stunned to find that the crowd preferred the release of Barabbas. Even so, he expected that the crowd might be mollified by a severe punishment of Jesus. Again, such was not the case, for when he asked what they expected him to do with Jesus, they called for His crucifixion. Trying to appeal to them for justice by asking what evil He had done proved to be totally ineffective. By this time the group had become a mob, and their chant "Crucify him" indicated to Pilate that a riot was in the making. Then Pilate called for a basin to wash his hands to indicate to the group that the blood of this innocent man would not be upon him. Matthew 27:25 indicates that the Jews accepted responsibility. Pilate then released Barabbas according to the expectation of the crowd, had Jesus scourged and delivered Him up to be crucified.

Once the verdict was rendered and it became obvious that Jesus was condemned to death, any sense of civility and restraint by the Romans was removed. The soldiers made sport of Jesus, probably not understanding much about the preceding events or the sentiments of Pilate. Crucifixion was not a rare activity so their behavior was probably ingrained from dozens of similar experiences. They stripped Jesus, mocked Him by placing a robe upon Him and giving Him a reed to serve as a scepter and knelt before Him hailing Him as King of the Jews. This was not so much a mockery of the man Jesus as it was an expression of the Romans' attitude toward the Jews in general. They found great delight in seeing this pathetic victim as the King of the Jews. Their sarcasm was not meant so much to be cruel as it was to be insulting of the Jewish nation. They began to spit at Jesus in their mockery.

After they had mocked Him, they led Him away to crucify Him. While they proceeded through the streets of Jerusalem by the longest route possible to the site of crucifixion, Jesus faltered under the load of the cross beam. The Roman soldiers pressed into service a man identified as Simon from Cyrene. This man was the one who would bear the cross of Jesus to Golgotha. Mark informs his audience that this Simon was the father of Alexander and Rufus, who apparently were persons well known to those who would have been Mark's readers. Individuals of those names are found in other places in the New Testament.

The Crucifixion of Jesus (Matthew 27:33-56)

Prior to proceeding further into the passion of Jesus it might be helpful to refer readers to a more thorough treatment of the events of the passion. In *The Broken God: Power under Control,*[5] I have written an entire chapter on each of the episodes of the passion based on Mark's account (the anointing in Bethany, the Last Supper, the garden prayer, the arrest, the Jewish trial, the Roman trial, the crucifixion, the burial and the resurrection.). The discussion of the crucifixion of Jesus in that book is fairly thorough and will not be recounted here in great detail.

The Gospels agree that Jesus was crucified at a place called Golgotha, which means "The Place of the Skull," perhaps because of the shape of the rock formation. Contemporary pilgrims to Jerusalem are often shown a place outside the city that has a rock formation resembling The Place of the Skull. Whether that is the exact location is impossible to determine. Arriving at the site, Jesus was offered a strong drink to dull His senses. This was the only humane action in the crucifixion process and most likely it was rendered by Jewish women. Jesus refused the drink when He realized what it was, probably so that He would experience the full wrath of the cup that He knew He would drink, namely, the cup of God's wrath.

The crucifixion itself included driving nails between the two arm bones in the wrist and securing the arms by rope. The cross beam was then hoisted to the upright beam, on which His feet were nailed. The impaled victim would hang suspended between earth and sky until He expired. Once Jesus was on the cross, the soldiers set about their normal routine during the hours of watch. They began dividing His garments and then cast lots for the outer garment so that it would not have to be divided.

Above every crucified victim the charge of his offense was posted. All four Gospels mention different wording of the charge, but they all have the words "King of the Jews." Matthew is probably right in mentioning that the personal name Jesus was part of the superscription. Two criminals were crucified with Jesus, one on either side of Him. They may have been associated with Barabbas, but their crime was less, as they are mentioned merely as robbers, not murderers.

Verses 39-44 indicate some of the events that occurred during the six hours Jesus was suspended prior to His death. Three groups mocked Jesus. First, those who were passing by the crucifixion site taunted Him for His claim to destroy the temple and rebuild it in three days. Their taunt was that if He could do such a mighty act, then He ought to be able to save Himself.

Second, not content with having their way in the crucifixion, the chief priests, elders and scribes continued their savagery by verbally abusing Jesus. They mocked Him for not being able to save

Himself even though He had saved others. Then
hailing Him as King of the Jews, they confessed
that if He would come down from the cross, they
would believe in Him. To their statement, "Come
down from the cross, if you are the Son of God"
(27:40), General William Booth once retorted, "It
is precisely because He would not come down
that we believe in Him."[6]

Third, the robbers who were being crucified on
both sides of Jesus were also casting insults at Jesus. Matthew shows no difference between the
two robbers, whereas Luke reports that one of the
robbers was repentant and was promised by Jesus
that he would enter paradise.

At noontime, the sixth hour, darkness came
upon the land and remained for three hours. At 3
P.M. Jesus cried out aloud, saying in Aramaic, " "
which means "My God, my God, why have you
forsaken me?" Some have suggested that the
sound of the words "*Eloi, Eloi*" was confusing to
those who heard it and they were supposing that
He was making an appeal to Elijah. This is unlikely. More likely is the possibility that those who
were standing there clearly understood what Jesus
was doing and thought that perhaps Jesus was im-
ploring God to send Elijah to His aid. The connection between Elijah and the Messiah was well
known by the Jews (see, for example, Malachi 4:5-
6). The crowd was eager to see whether or not Elijah would come to rescue Jesus (Matthew 27:49).

After this Jesus cried out with a loud voice and
yielded up His spirit. Matthew communicates

clearly, that Jesus voluntarily laid down His life (see John 10:18). The words in Luke 23:46 indicate that Jesus said, "Father, into your hands I commit my spirit," and John 19:30 adds that Jesus also said, "It is finished."

Immediately following Jesus' last words and last breath, several cosmic occurrences began. The earth shook in such a way that many rocks were split. This earthquake may have been the cause of the veil of the temple being torn in two. On the other hand, the rending of the veil of the temple may have been unrelated to the earthquake. Tombs were opened because of the earthquake and the bodies of many saints were raised, came out of the tombs, and appeared to many in the holy city (Matthew 27:52-53). Matthew is the only evangelist who recorded this astonishing event. The way the episode is reported causes much confusion. The earthquake seems to have been the cause of the rocks being split open and the tombs being opened. However, the bodies of the saints were not raised out of their tombs until after the resurrection of Jesus. The word translated "resurrection" in verse 53 occurs nowhere else in the New Testament. The usual word is avoided by the evangelist here in favor of a word that in classical Greek refers to something being raised up, without substantial change.

Most likely, the saints are Old Testament believers and others who, like Simeon, Anna, Zacharias and Elizabeth, had trusted in God's Messiah for their salvation. The precise mission of these saints who were raised up for a time is not made clear. Nor are we told about their subsequent existence. Did they return to their tombs? Were they resurrected with Jesus for a special ascension? Did they accompany Jesus prior to the descent into Hades? Much mystery continues to cloud these cosmic events.

The astonishing events evoked belief by the centurion who was keeping guard over Jesus. The earthquake and darkness were probably the events that caused him to declare that Jesus was truly the Son of God, or a son of God. The language does not clearly indicate the depth of the centurion's insight. For future purposes in this story, Matthew reported that many women were watching the events from a distance. Among them were Mary Magdalene, Mary the mother of James and Joseph (also the mother of Jesus) and the mother of James and John the sons of Zebedee, who had come from Galilee to minister to Jesus.

The Burial of Jesus (Matthew 27:57-66)

Consistent with the other Gospel writers, Matthew reported that a wealthy man from Arimathea named Joseph, who was a member of the Sanhedrin (Mark 15:43), volunteered to show respect for the corpse of Jesus. Matthew indicates that he had become a disciple of Jesus (Matthew 27:57). Because Joseph was not a blood relative of Jesus, the law required that he must obtain permission to receive the body of Jesus. So he went to Pilate and made his request, which Pilate approved. The complexity of receiving this permission was not recorded by Matthew but by Mark, who indicated that Pilate was surprised that Jesus was already dead. Prior to giving permission for Joseph to take the body, the governor sent a centurion to verify the death of the victim. This little detail has discredited the so-called swoon theory, which attempted to cast doubt on the resurrection by claiming that Jesus never really died.

Once he received the body, Joseph with the aid of Nicodemus (John 19:39) wrapped the body with a mixture of myrrh and aloes and then laid it in his own new tomb which had been hewn out of a rock. Then they rolled a large stone over the entrance of the tomb. Matthew reports that two of the women, both named Mary, were sitting opposite the grave watching this event.

On the following day the Pharisees and chief priests went to Pilate to request that the grave be made more secure. They had remembered that Jesus claimed He would rise after three days. The Jewish leaders were concerned that the disciples of Jesus would come and steal the dead body and then spread the rumor that Jesus had risen from the dead. They were concerned that the final deception would be worse than the first. Pilate indulged their request, telling them to use their own temple guard and make it as secure as they knew how. The Jews then did exactly that by assigning a guard duty and applying a seal on the stone that covered the tomb.

The Resurrection of Jesus (Matthew 28:1-15)

With the Sabbath ending at sundown on the last day of the week, the Jewish people were free to resume normal activity. This prompted Mary Magdalene and the other Mary to travel early toward dawn of the first day of the week to look at the grave. A second earthquake had occurred according to Matthew 28:2. No comment is made at this point in the narrative about the presence of dead saints walking around, but the phrase in 27:53 states that they came out of the tombs after His resurrection, so it must have been this earthquake that opened the tombs. Possibly, Matthew, in recording the phenomenal cosmic events that occurred when Jesus died, wanted all those events to be seen together. In any case, the earthquake described in 28:2 was called a severe earthquake and may have been caused by the angel who descended from heaven and rolled away the stone from the tomb. The two Marys found the angel sitting on the stone, appearing in a brilliance that was described like lightning and as white as snow. The two Marys were not the only ones to see the angel, because verse 4 indicates that the temple guards who had been posted "were so afraid of him that they shook and became like dead men." The two Marys did not lose consciousness, for the angel ministered to them by telling them not to fear. He then indicated that he knew they were looking for Jesus and told them that Jesus had indeed risen. The angel then invited the Marys to visit the place where Jesus had lain. Whether they did that was not told by Matthew. The angel's next command was that they hasten to find the disciples to tell them that Jesus had risen from the dead and that He would meet them in Galilee as He had earlier foretold. Matthew reports that the two Marys then departed quickly from the tomb, filled with fear and joy, running to report the event to the disciples.

As they were traveling, Jesus met them and greeted them. Matthew did not report that the Marys had difficulty recognizing Him. Rather, they took hold of His feet and began to worship Him. No doubt they were still filled with fear. Jesus gave the same reassuring words that the angel gave, "Do not be afraid." Then He repeated the commission given by the angels.

By this time the nearly comatose guards recovered and went into the city to report the events to the chief priests. The Jewish leaders convened to decide what to do about the difficult position in which they found themselves. Presumably, the information that we have of this episode may well be from the same source as the information about the rendering of the veil of the temple (28:51) and the securing of the tomb (28:62-66), namely, the priests who became Christians (see Acts 6:7, "a large number of priests became obedient to the faith"). This attempt to explain the disappearance of the body of Jesus was somewhat successful in that the Jews dispersed this story among their own people. Matthew reported that it is still believed by many "to this very day" (Matthew 28:15).

The Great Commission (Matthew 28:16-20)

The rendezvous in Galilee succeeded. Jesus met the disciples at a designated place. Their response was immediate worship. According to Matthew, some remained doubtful, however, as we may well imagine. The people of the first century no more expected to see a dead man walking around than would we in the 20th century. Unlike the other Gospels, which report other appearances and activity of Jesus in His pre-ascension days, Matthew simply gives the final commissioning in which Jesus assured His disciples that all authority had now been committed to Him in heaven and on earth. The victory of His resurrection was the final vindication of His claim to be the Son of God. Their responsibility in the light of this knowledge is to make disciples of all the nations. Making disciples would include two specific activities: first, baptizing these new disciples in the name of the Father, Son and Holy Spirit; and, second, teaching them to obey the commands of Jesus. Matthew's Gospel ends with a final reassurance of His presence: "And surely I am with you always, to the very end of the age" (Matthew 28:19).

As disciples of Jesus continue to obey this great commission, Matthew in glory may yet have opportunity to write a sequel to his gospel of the kingdom. Perhaps as he frequently did, he will write about the fulfillment of an Old Testament

Scripture, such as:

> In my vision at night I looked, and there
> before me was one like a son of man, coming
> with the clouds of heaven. He approached
> the Ancient of Days and was led into his
> presence. He was given authority, glory and
> sovereign power; all peoples, nations and
> men of every language worshiped him. His
> dominion is an everlasting dominion that
> will not pass away, and his kingdom is one
> that will never be destroyed. (Daniel 7:13-
> 14)

Endnotes

1. Alfred Plummer, *An Exegetical Commentary on
   The Gospel According to St. Matthew* (Grand Rapids: Baker Book House, 1982), p. 357.
2. Plummer, p. 362.
3. Ibid., p. 362, footnote 2.
4. Ibid., pp. 379-380.
5. David E. Schroeder, *The Broken God: Power Under Control* (Grand Rapids, MI: Baker Book
   House, 1994).
6. William Barclay, *The Gospel of Matthew*, Vol. 2
   (Philadelphia: The Westminster Press, 1958),
   p. 405.